A Comprehensive Beginner's Guide To

Crystals & Healing Stones

Including Intuitive Guidance, Experiential Knowledge, & Practical Therapies

Sharon Stone

INTUITIVE WAY

Intuitive Way Publishing
A division of Hedhaus Inc
158F Briarwynd Court
Edmonton, AB, Canada
T5T0H4
www.intuitive-way.com

Table of Contents

Special Bonus!

These two bonus books are yours for free!

 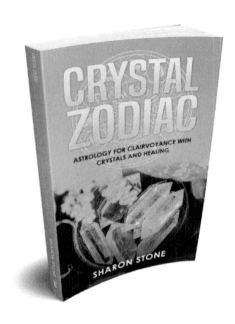

Yes, <u>FREE</u>!

Get exclusive access right now to these and more by joining our online community.
Just scan the QR code below with your phone camera!

About the Author

Sharon Stone was born and raised in Montreal, Quebec, to a family of healers. She received her M.Ed. degree in 2001, after which she lived abroad for five years in Japan. There, she taught English to school children.

After being diagnosed with cancer in 2006, Sharon immersed herself in alternative medicine to avoid harmful chemotherapy. With a mixture of crystal therapies, Reiki, and herbal medicines, Sharon began to change her life, and in 2009, she awoke to a diagnosis of remission and has been cancer-free since. Her thorough knowledge base in these therapies, background in teaching, and passion for helping others to heal led Sharon to share her faith with the world in written form.

Married with two children, Sharon now lives in Austin, Texas with her husband of nine years.

Introduction

"Let us carve gems out of our stony hearts, and let them light our path to love."[1]
Rumi

Alternative healing therapies emphasize our intuitive nature and our remarkably human ability to apply compassion to ourselves and others. This book, *Crystals and Healing Stones*, offers practical therapies through intuitive pathways that are easy for the complete beginner to follow and comprehend.

I am writing this book today, not because I am myself a master of alternative medicine—far from it. I am a lifelong student with a passion for teaching, and this book is a measure of love, not mastery. I wanted to write a comprehensive guide to crystal healing that relies on *your intuition* so that you can confidently practice these therapies on your own, without the need for expensive professional treatments—and I was called to do this because I know how powerful these therapies are, myself.

I grew up in a family of health professionals: my father was a family doctor and my mother an emergency room nurse. From a very young age, I was made aware of all the things that can go wrong with a person's health. I remember Mom coming home exhausted and wiry after long hours. I would stay awake at night and listen to her cry into my father's shoulder after particularly harrowing experiences in the ER. Dad doted upon me, treating my every childhood scrape and bruise. He imparted to me the importance of preventative care and healthy living—which, in combination with my mother's horror stories, stuck with me.

I have always been the type to take rigorous care of my good health: I watched what I ate, exercised five times a week, practiced good hygiene, and took my medications as prescribed. So when I was diagnosed with cancer in 2006, the news positively floored me. How could this have happened—to *me* of all people, when I wasn't even thirty years old? I had never smoked in my life, I hardly drank, and I ate all of my vegetables, just like Dad taught me to. I felt like the universe was playing a cruel joke on me, and my faith in traditional medicine was seriously shaken.

I was also living alone abroad at the time and, faced with the prospect of moving home just to die in a hospital bed, one thing became certain: I did not want to resort to barraging my body with chemotherapy and radiation therapy until all other options had been explored. Of course, my medically-minded parents wanted to keep me alive at *any* cost—but is a life of misery and pain truly one worth living? Being so young, I decided it wasn't.

And so, I surprised myself and my parents. I decided to stay abroad in Japan and seek alternative healing therapies. Yes, I sought treatment from and eventually studied under Reiki practitioners, took ancient Eastern herbal remedies, but ultimately everything changed when I harnessed the healing power of crystal therapies.

Miraculously, the growth of my cancer slowed to a halt. Without either surgery or chemotherapy, I was declared cancer-free. My Dad had to eat his own words.

One thing that alternative therapies have taught me is the importance of taking care of not only your body but your mind and soul, as well. Traditional Western medicine treats these three as distinct units—and importantly, it doesn't concern itself with the spiritual *at all*.

I still believe in Western medicine, and I would never advocate that you take advice from this or any other book over the word of your doctor. I am glad that my parents gave me all of my vaccinations and treated my childhood injuries; crystals can't prevent polio or properly set a fractured tibia. But traditional medicine simply doesn't treat patients *holistically*.

In the years since my diagnosis, I've come to understand that perhaps I wasn't as healthy pre-cancer as I thought I was. Sure, I ate well and exercised, but spiritually? I ran on empty. I've come to believe that crystals and other alternative therapies were successful for me precisely because they treated the illness at its source—in my heart and soul.

This is the true power of energy healing, and in this book, you'll learn about the healing properties of each stone for the spiritual as well as the physical.

If you are anything like I was, you currently stand at a precipice, eager to receive the wonders of natural healing—but you're missing the essential puzzle pieces to build your own practice. This book will mark the beginning of your simple solution; comprehensive knowledge to bridge the gap between you and your self-care goals.

My goal with this book is not to fool you into thinking you will suddenly be filled with immaculate healing powers after purchasing your first crystals. Instead, whether or not you believe in alternative medicines, I aim to show you that energy is indeed malleable and can be channeled to alleviate our human suffering. My goal is to inspire optimism in you, the reader, and my hope is that you will use the therapies in this book as a way to express your own self-love and love for others.

The book will guide you on your healing journey, teaching you how to use your own intuition to utilize crystals for healing all that may ail you. Through this straightforward guide, you will become sufficient in the vocabulary and terminology of crystal healing and learn specific therapies you can apply to yourself at home. During your journey, you will accumulate crystals and stones to match the recommendations I've prescribed for particular ailments and from this begin to form your own personal healing practice. As you experiment with different methods of using and interacting with your crystal collection, you will gain confidence in your own intuitive abilities; health and prosperity will be at your fingertips.

I am excited to accompany you on this journey! Shall we begin?

Part I

Foundational Knowledge: Everything You Need to Get into Crystal Healing

Chapter One
The Power of Crystals: Healing Mind, Body, and Spirit

"In a crystal, we have clear evidence of the existence of a formative life-principle, and though we cannot understand the life of a crystal, it is nonetheless a living being."

Nikola Tesla[2]

I am eager to share with you all I've learned about crystal healing so that you can use crystals to help you take control of your life and change your own story for the better. Before we learn about crystal therapies, though, we must begin with some foundational knowledge: what exactly *are* crystals, and why should you put your faith in them?

In this chapter, we will explore these questions and find some fascinating facts about crystals.

Crystallography 101

A crystal is a naturally-occurring mineral formation in which the atoms that comprise the mineral are arranged in a specific molecular pattern called a lattice.

As a result of its particular atomic structure, each crystal has an unchanging, stable energy pattern and vibrational frequency, giving the crystal its unique essence. By embracing this essence, we can harness the power of these ancient pieces of Earth to enhance and transform our human energy, which by nature is unstable, changing constantly as we interact with others.

Sharon Stone

The study of crystals is called crystallography, and it involves a lot of physics and chemistry. We won't get *too* into the weeds here with the scientific stuff, but understanding the building blocks of crystals will help us later when we talk about their individual healing properties—and it reveals a lot about their beautiful, crystalline shapes.

Crystalline Structure

A crystal is defined by its structure; without this structure, it wouldn't be a crystal at all. A fascinating fact: the atomic arrangement of a mineral is often reflected in its crystalline shape (also called crystal habit) on a macro scale. It's like a fractal; the same pattern keeps repeating and repeating as the crystal grows; what we see and hold is a reflection of its molecular structure.

These patterns, which define the physical structure of crystals, are called crystal lattices or crystal systems. We can represent these systems on paper using circles for atoms and lines for the bonds that tie them together. What makes each crystal in a system unique—what separates smoky quartz from rose quartz, in other words—are the specific atoms that fill in the "circles" of the lattice.

Like the seven chakras, there are seven primary crystal systems, each producing unique crystal shapes:

System	*Shape & Properties*	*Examples*	
Cubic	Cubic crystals are shaped like cubes and octahedrons. As a class, these crystals represent stability and regularity, making them powerful physical healers.	**Fluorite**	**Pyrite**
Hexagonal	Hexagonal systems produce crystals shaped like double pyramids, double-sided pyramids, and four-sided pyramids. These are great for focusing healing on the specific area in need.	**Apatite**	**Quartz**

System	Shape & Properties	Examples	
Monoclinic	Monoclinic systems create crystals shaped like pinacoids and prisms. These crystals have a pulsing unidirectional energy.	**Azurite**	**Selenite**
Orthorhombic	Orthorhombic crystals are shaped like pyramids, double pyramids, rhombic pyramids, and pinacoids. These crystals are perfect for clearing unwanted or negative energies.	**Celestite**	**Topaz**
Tetragonal	Tetragonal systems produce crystals shaped like double and eight-sided pyramids, four-sided prisms, and trapezohedrons. As a class, these crystals are highly adaptable and useful for transforming energy.	**Wulfenite**	**Apophyllite**
Triclinic	This lattice type has either no symmetry at all or a single point of symmetry, i.e., two parallel sides. As a class, these crystals have harmonizing and integrating properties.	**Labradorite**	**Turquoise**

System	Shape & Properties	Examples	
Trigonal 	With crystals shaped like three-sided pyramids and rhombohedrons, trigonal crystals are balancing and re-energizing.	**Calcite**	**Tourmaline**

The Many Shapes of Crystals

While every crystal has a crystalline structure, it's not always obvious at the macro scale. To illustrate, here are two different pyrite crystals:

One of these is very obviously "cubic," while the other looks kind of like an amorphous blob. If you were to look at the second piece of pyrite with a magnifying glass, you'd see that many of those glittering, shimmery bits in the blob are actually tiny crystalline cubes.

Stones that have formed like this with many tiny, individual crystals melded together are referred to as "microcrystalline." Microcrystalline stones include geodes and other fossils. They are what you commonly buy in a gem store as polished stones. In some stones, the crystal structure is completely unobservable to the naked eye, as with a natural lump of turquoise—these are called "cryptocrystalline" stones.

Every crystal has a tendency to break in a specific way when enough force is applied. Crystallographers refer to this as a crystal's cleavage, and it can have a big impact on the shape of a crystal. Take, for example, these two pieces of fluorite:

8

The first crystal is displaying its cubic habit in all its natural glory. The second crystal is not shaped like a cube but like an eight-sided die. What happened? The second crystal is a piece of a larger fluorite crystal. When fluorite breaks off, it does so on these specific octahedral planes, creating fluorite "dice."

The Magic of Crystallization

Crystals form in nature through a process known as crystallization, in which molecules gather together and stabilize in a crystal lattice as a liquid mineral cools and begins to harden into a solid. Crystallization occurs when magma or lava hardens as well as when water evaporates from a liquid mixture, leaving behind only mineral components—this is what happens when fossils and geodes are formed. Crystals start off small and grow larger in a repetitive pattern as more molecules join together through the crystallization process. The duration of time depends on the crystal, which establishes its rarity—amethyst geodes take millions of years, while quartz can form in as little as hours or days.

Beginnings Deep Beneath Our Feet

There is something truly profound and magical about the formation of crystals deep within the Earth, taking place over millennia.

Beneath our feet lies the Earth's crust, the cooled, solid layer of rock that makes up the surface of the planet. The crust is as thick as 25 miles deep in some places beneath the seabed. Beneath it lies the mantle, which comprises a solid 80% of the Earth's volume and measures nearly 2,000 miles thick. Unlike the crust, the mantle is not entirely solid: it consists mainly of magma, viscous and fiery orange-red liquid rock composed of many different minerals. When this magma pushes through the crust of the Earth to erupt onto the surface, we call it lava.

The place where the Earth's solid crust meets its liquid mantle is a dynamic one, full of constant movement and change—powerfully transformative. Under extremely high pressures and temperatures, rock in the Earth's crust breaks off and crumbles, melting into the surrounding mantle and changing its mineral composition. Magma, meanwhile, rushes in to fill nooks and crannies left in the solid earth. As it begins to cool, this mineral-rich magma starts to crystallize, forming crystals in all the cracks and fissures.

Natural Variations

While new crystals coalesce in these cavities within the Earth's crust, the dynamic environment rages on around them. Passageways in the rock open and collapse again as tectonic plates shift and more mantle meets more crust, allowing crystal growth to stop and restart. This stop-and-go process often leaves a mark on the crystals, including color variations caused by impurities, twinning effects, phantom effects, different minerals growing on the same crystal, and more.

The Ancient History of Crystal Healing

Human beings have been fascinated with stones and minerals from the beginning of our history. 30,000-year-old amulets made of Baltic amber have been discovered in British gravesites, and the distance that amber traveled to be buried there indicates how revered these amulets must have been by their wearers.

The oldest known written reference to the use of crystals for something other than jewelry comes from the ancient Sumerians who used them to practice magic. The ancient Egyptians favored lapis lazuli, turquoise, emerald, and carnelian for amulets designed to encourage protection and health. The ancient Greeks studied crystals alongside mathematics and philosophy; they attributed many properties to crystals and named many of the stones referenced in this book. In fact, the word "crystal" comes from the Greek word meaning *ice*, as the Greeks believed clear quartz to be made of permanently frozen water. Greek soldiers rubbed hematite stones on their bodies for invulnerability in battle, and sailors likewise wore agate amulets for protection out in Poseidon's perilous sea. Jade, of course, was highly prized in ancient China, where it has long been recognized as a healing stone, particularly for the kidneys.

Much of this ancient knowledge was lost or repressed during the dark ages, when the Christian church outlawed alternative healing and divinatory practices as heretical. Later, in the age of enlightenment, man turned his nose up at crystals in favor of medical advancements.

It wasn't until the 1970s and 80s that crystal healing as we know it today was brought back to the mainstream as part of the new age revolution. Today's crystal healing therapies cross the boundaries of religious belief—they are widely accepted not as fringe culture but as a therapy complimentary to modern medical treatments.

How It Works: Vibrational Frequencies & Energy Fields

"If you want to find the secrets of the universe, think in terms of energy, frequency, and vibration," said Nikola Tesla.[3]

Recall that crystals have a specific patterned atomic structure. Scientifically, The Law of Vibration states that everything in the universe is, in its most basic, purest form, made of energy—and that energy resonates at a vibratory frequency. Atoms and molecules vibrate—and so, by virtue of its crystalline atomic structure in which patterns are repeated over and over again, a crystal's vibrations are especially *stable*, which makes them especially powerful to us.

When you place a crystal over your body or close to you, it's innately stable energy interacts with your own energy fields to promote physical, emotional, and spiritual cleansing. Think of a crystal as an energy magnet, absorbing negative vibrations from your body and spirit and replacing them with the crystal's characteristic energy. Like other energy-based therapies, healing crystals work by channeling your own internal energy levels, thus harmonizing your cells from the inside out.

Quartz Crystal: The Master Healer

Modern science backs the ability of crystals to transform, amplify, and transmit energies, and a perfect example of this is the powerful quartz crystal.

Quartz is the most abundant mineral on the Earth's surface and an essential constituent of the ground beneath your feet pretty much anywhere you stand in the world. It's chemical composition is silicon dioxide, SiO_2, with one molecule of silicone for every two of oxygen in its crystal lattice, and it's unique properties make it one of the most useful substances on earth, from beach sand to advanced electronic devices.

Quartz is an electronic miracle because when it is bent or compressed, it generates voltage on its surface; this is referred to as a piezoelectric effect. Piezoelectricity is the electric charge that accumulates in a solid material, and like quartz, this same energy is found in biological materials like our bones—and the very DNA in our cells.

Almost no energy is lost within a quartz crystal. If there were a bell shaped from a single crystal of quartz, it would continue to sound for several minutes after you rang it. This is the vibrational power of the master healing stone. It harmonizes with an extremely high frequency and is capable of channeling this elevated energy into the physical realm.

I hope that what you've found in this introduction to the world of healing crystals and stones is enlightening. You should be intrigued to learn how you can harness the vibrational frequencies of crystals for your own benefit and the benefit of your loved ones!

In the next chapter, I'll lay out everything you need to know to build your own crystal collection—and *use* it. That last bit is key. You can seek out and buy all the rarest and most beautiful crystals—great geodes of amethyst, shining moldavite pendants, immaculate moonstone spheres—spending thousands of dollars to collect each and every stone for its specific powers. Still, if you don't know how to *harness* their energies, your rare crystals may be nothing but expensive paperweights.

Have no fear. The intuitive approach I'll teach you in this book will ensure you can confidently choose and apply crystals to treat any ailment.

Chapter Two
A Crystal Collection of Your Own

Collecting crystals is a fun and rewarding endeavor, and I'm sure you are eager to get started building your own set. Perhaps you have questions like: "How do I heal my insomnia?" "What about my cancer?" "My father complains of his ulcers," or, "My son sometimes gets diarrhea."

Well, the varieties of crystal you start with will lead you to methods for alleviating all this suffering. Perhaps you have a small but growing collection already, and want to put it to use with expert precision—or maybe you are teaching someone what to do with crystals, aside from admiring their beauty on your shelf.

In this chapter, we'll discuss everything you need to know not only to build a personalized crystal collection but to make the most of it, promoting healing and wellness in every aspect of your life.

A Beginner's Collection

In the next part of the book, you'll find a detailed reference guide to more than 60 of the most essential healing crystals to have in your collection. But where to start?

Here is a brief description of the top 10 crystals I recommend in any collection, all of them are relatively accessible and inexpensive, and each possesses healing qualities you will want to have on hand:

Stone	*Major Properties*
Clear Quartz	The master healer, clear quartz is essential in any collection as its applications are virtually limitless. With its extremely high vibrational frequency, quartz crystal has a powerful cleansing and balancing power on the body and mind.
Amethyst	Amethyst, like many other healing crystals, is actually a variety of quartz mineral. Known as the crystal of sobriety, amethyst has powerful mental and emotional healing powers. It can put you in touch with your own intuitive powers and balance the crown chakra.
Tiger's Eye	This powerfully protective stone promotes willpower and confidence, stabilizes mood swings, and dispels anxiety, fear, and pain from the mind and body.
Rose Quartz	Yet another essential variety of quartz, rose quartz is a highly spiritual stone that represents unconditional love. As it purifies and opens the emotional heart, so too it cleanses and heals the physical heart.
Selenite	Selenite opens the crown chakra. A powerful healer and cleanser, it helps to align the spinal column and can reduce the effects of free radicals, fighting cancer at its source.

Stone		*Major Properties*
Carnelian		This warmly colored stone promotes kidney function and heals the lower back. It is also used to ease arthritis and depression and to aid in overcoming abuse.
Aquamarine		This calming stone quiets a restless mind and promotes inner peace. Used to treat thyroid problems, it helps regulate all manner of hormones and boosts the immune system.
Moonstone		Moonstone stabilizes emotions and promotes intuition. Used to treat digestive problems, it removes toxins from the body and stimulates the pineal gland—excellent for pregnancy and childbirth.
Hematite		Known as the "stone of the mind," hematite is excellent for mental acumen. This grounding and protective stone dispels negativity, balances energies, and promotes equilibrium between the spiritual and physical selves. Used to treat blood disorders.
Citrine		Another quartz variety, powerfully energizing, sunny citrine recharges and refreshes body, mind, and spirit. It treats chemical imbalances and reverses degenerative diseases.

Crystals to Avoid as a Beginner

So these are some good crystals to start with—what about crystals you should avoid as a beginner? In truth, there is no good blanket statement regarding crystals to be avoided. Each crystal has its own purpose, and if it calls to you, heed it. The most danger you are in is perhaps encouraging unintended effects or combining opposing crystals in such a way that their effects are canceled out; the encyclopedia in Chapter 3 will be a big help for you in avoiding these conflicting energies.

You may have heard horror stories about people whose lives were turned upside down when they added a rare mineral known as moldavite to their collections. Moldavite is not harmful or hurtful. All crystals have benevolent energies, and it is in *our* hands that misfortune can occur. Still, rare moldavite possesses powerful qualities that can be unnerving to the inexperienced.

Another good reason to avoid a crystal is if it's hard to find or expensive. Stick with what's accessible until you've got a good handle on your basic collection; then, you can branch out into rarities.

Harmonizing yourself with the ten common stones above might reveal what kind of quagmire you find yourself in—emotionally, mentally, and spiritually. I, for one, realized I wasn't invincible, and with the use of amethyst, I began to sleep and dream better—even experiencing astral dreams.

Let the Crystal Choose You

While the above list is an excellent starting point, in truth, when choosing your crystals, you should rely on your intuition and choose the crystals that speak to you. In fact, many crystal healers might say that you don't choose the crystal; the crystal chooses *you*. Your body and spirit respond to the vibrational frequencies of those crystals that stir something in your imagination, your soul; this is your cue, your sign from the universe, that the healing you need is right in front of you.

Here is a simple guide to choosing crystals intuitively in a gem shop.

If you don't have access to a brick and mortar store, choosing crystals intuitively may be a bit harder without your sense of touch—but the concept is generally the same. Flip ahead to Chapters 3 and 4, and let your intuition guide you through the pages. Choose a crystal whose description and photo speaks to you.

Set Your Intention

Before you step foot in a crystal shop, take a moment to yourself in a quiet space. Close your eyes, breathe in deeply, ground yourself, and set your intention for this step in your crystal healing journey.

This intention doesn't have to be long or involved; it can be as simple as one word that speaks to you. It may be a wide-open and general intention (such as, "Let my spirit guides point me to the crystal I need right now,") or something specific (like, "I will heal my broken heart"). Once you've settled on an intention, keep your eyes closed and repeat it to yourself a few times to commit it to memory.

An essential step is to keep a journal, and write your intentions down in it! If you don't have a journal of your own, I've included lined pages at the end of the book you can use to record intentions, affirmations, and more.

Let Your Spirit Guide You

With your intention determined, it's time to head to the gem store! Make a point to go in with an open mind and leave your judgment and expectations at the door.

Walk around the shop and take it in with all your senses. Touch stones with your fingertips and hold them in your hands (if they are not behind a glass case—and if they are, the shop attendants would be happy to help you). Let your spirit guide you; let go and trust in your intuitive powers. Repeat your intention to yourself, and trust that when you find the right crystal, you will know it.

Here are some signs to look out for as you shop intuitively.

- Does a specific crystal catch your eye with its beauty? Does the color call to you? What does it say?
- Does a specific crystal jog your memory, reminding you of someone or something important? Does it call to mind the intention you set?
- When you touch a crystal, can you feel it tingle in your hand? Can you feel it radiate heat or coolness through your body? Can you sense its vibrations?
- When you touch a crystal, does it bring up a powerful emotion in you? Do you feel a certain way when you look at it?
- Does the texture of a stone feel "right" under your fingertips? When you pick it up, do you have an urge to steal it as your own?

The possibilities are nearly endless here, limited only by your imagination. Use these questions as a guide to practice using your intuition, but ultimately, trust whatever it is about a crystal that speaks to you. If a stone feels "right" in your hands, don't let it go; buy it, bring it home, and allow its energies to positively impact your life.

If you're not accustomed to tuning in to your intuition for guidance like this, you may be tempted to bring a friend with you to the gem shop. While having company is OK, making your own choice is absolutely vital—it is the first step to bridging the gap between intuition and hesitancy.

Don't worry; the hesitancy is normal! Each of us has a different level of sensitivity to the energies and vibrations that crystals make us aware of. The more you work with them, the stronger you will build the awareness of your own frequencies and how crystals interact with your energy field. Be gentle with yourself and take your time shopping before you leave. With practice and patience, you will find a sense of protection embodied in every stone.

Keep Your Crystals Close

Wearing your crystals is a great way to make daily use of your collection. Beyond the many beautiful varieties of natural stone jewelry there are to choose from, there are ways to wear simple palm stones and small crystals on your body, keeping you in direct contact with the crystal's healing vibrations throughout your day or night.

When used therapeutically and with focused intent, the frequency of a crystal puts the body's energy systems in balance and stimulates natural healing processes. They pass their healing energies to us, raising our own vibrations to higher levels, which is best accomplished through direct contact—thus, wearing crystals is truly the best way to realize their healing properties for yourself.

For instance, I wore hematite around my neck as an amulet to invoke alpha brain wave patterns. Hematite promoted clear thoughts in me as the "stone of the mind." I enjoyed keeping it close to my skin as it was very grounding, evoking deeper thoughts, stronger memory, and helping me with my vertigo while hiking mountains.

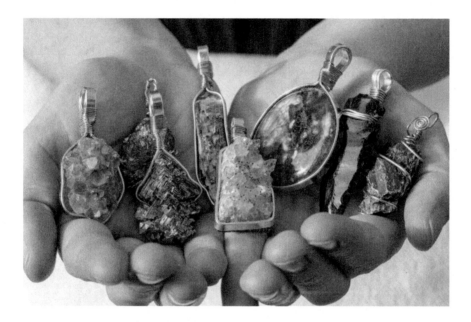

Figure 1: A selection of hand-wrapped raw crystal pendants.

Gem & Crystal Jewelry

Jewelry is a popular and pretty way to wear stones. Yes, even the diamonds in your wedding band or your grandmother's pearl earrings possess unique healing and spiritual properties. These precious and semi-precious gemstones are crystals prized for their cut, clarity, and purity. An increasingly popular option is natural stone jewelry; these stones are commonly judged on their luster, color, and natural shape, and they often come hand-wrapped in wire rather than in gold settings (see Figure 1).

You can find artisanal jewelry, beaded bracelets, elegantly wire-wrapped amulets, engraved rings, pendulum necklaces, and more when you search online. The choice is yours, then—because coming to peace with your healing journey ultimately involves submitting to the properties of the crystals. I know I found use of beaded bracelets! When I wore my rose quartz while teaching, it helped to support my circulation system, and I felt less tired.

Crystal Cage Necklaces

My number-one piece of advice for your crystal collection is to purchase a crystal cage necklace. These simple hemp or wire pendants are flexible, allowing you to swap out the stone in the cage as you please. This way, you can utilize all the small crystals in your collection as jewelry, which will not only expand your options but bring you to love stone jewelry.

You can often find these cage necklaces for sale at stone shops and metaphysical healing shops. You can also find them for sale on Amazon. I used my cage necklace as I said before with hematite, and would switch to moonstone as soon as I began to feel inspired toward new beginnings and imminent success.

Pockets Full of Crystals

While nowhere near as glamorous as jewelry, carrying crystals in your pockets is a simple way to keep them in close contact and receive their healing benefits. At the start of each day, you may choose two or three small stones and place them in the pocket of your pants, shirt, or jacket. This is especially a great option for kids!

If you don't have any pockets, tuck the stones into your socks. It isn't unheard of that some women wear their crystals in their bras, although in that case, you're better off sticking to nicely polished stones! I must admit, without shame, I used selenite this way—one of the most powerful crystals. I would charge my Selenite every night in a sage smudge, and place it in a salted dish while I slept. I still do to this day, and my husband enjoys it. I would also use selenite to charge my other crystals—more on that later in this chapter!

Crystals Under Your Pillow

I highly recommend sleeping with a crystal under your pillow. This way, you can reap the benefits of its vibrations passively while you sleep—that's hours of uninterrupted healing.

Be mindful of your choice in crystal, though, as some have effects on sleep and dreams that you may not intend. For instance, ametrine promotes lucid dreaming, while labradorite is bound to awaken higher levels of consciousness, perhaps leading to prophetic dreams or messages from the universe. Again, an astral experience can be found with the help of any crystal—use your intuition to guide yourself.

Crystals Around the Home

While the direct contact you get when you wear crystals is a big boon to healing, it's simply not practical to wear every crystal in your collection every day. What to do with those you aren't wearing?

Keeping crystals around your living space is not only a beautiful way to decorate your home, but it comes with healing benefits. Much like your aura, which is the atmosphere you generate around yourself, stones that sit out in your home radiate energy into the environment. Of course, concentrating this healing on your body is one way to benefit, but by placing a crystal in your home, you are not the only beneficiary of the crystal's healing powers—it will promote energy flow in your home and impart some of its specific frequency on all who enter its presence.

Figure 2: A crystal altar on a nightstand, with amethyst and selenite to promote sleep and spiritual dreams.

I am convinced of the powerful healing properties of crystals and stones in the home, and so I want to share with you the method of organization I learned for displaying them in various places. I also offer justification based on the effects these crystals provide.

- **On your nightstand:** Crystals placed on your bedside table will have a similar effect as those placed under your pillow. As the bastion of your life in bed, it is best to stick with calming and sleep-inducing crystals, here: rose quartz, amethyst, and moonstone are all solid options, but of course, be mindful— moonstone does encourage pregnancy! See the beautiful example in Figure 2.
- **By the front door:** Crystals for wellbeing and protection are best placed at the entryway of your home. Use rose quartz to welcome love and prosperity into your home and tiger's eye to ward off any negative energies that may enter.
- **In the kitchen:** Add a pop of natural color to your kitchen shelf or windowsill with crystals. Energizing and uplifting citrine is a great choice.

- **In the living room:** Your living space is an excellent place to collect crystals. Line your bookshelves with them or add them to your coffee table centerpiece. I recommend aquamarine to encourage conversation and improve communication.
- **In the kids' rooms:** Hematite grounds and calms, excellent for toddlers (and anyone who needs a little help managing big emotions). It can also prevent nightmares.
- **Around the bathtub:** Clear quartz is a great option since it is highly stimulating to the immune system. You should know that our immune system is responsible for flushing out toxic agents and free radicals from our body, which pairs well with the bath and washroom.
- **In the study:** I found tiger's eye helps me to remain objective without clouding my emotions, permitting deep work when kept next to my computer. As you may know, social media can be a monster of negative energy, so I balance my tiger's eye with carnelian to protect me from the barrage of intense online programming.

Only 10 Crystals, Already So Much Healing!

So you've already found yourself immersed in the world of crystal healing with only 10 crystals in your collection. You'll naturally want to explore more and more ways to incorporate crystals into your life every day. The possibilities are endless! Here are some creative ideas to start:

- **Make a crystal altar:** Being a little more intentional with your collection is appropriate. Just think, why not create a crystal altar? Your altar will become a reference point for elaborations of your intentions. I found mine to be a laboratory for clearer thoughts and more stable emotions. Use an undisturbed surface in your home and cleanse it of errant energies with selenite. Then, arrange your choice of crystals based on your intention. You can add other objects, like photographs, candles, found items from nature, or precious keepsakes. Return to this altar at least once a day and be grateful for your intention. Feel the energies of the crystals on your altar and let them radiate out to you and throughout your home. If someone reminds you of your altar during your day, this is a good sign that you are meeting your intention.
- **Use a crystal grid:** Crystal grids combine sacred geometry with the healing energy of crystals; after all, what's more geometric than a crystal lattice? You can purchase a mat or a block with a printed or engraved image on it at a crystal shop or off the internet. Then, use your intuition to place crystals on the various points indicated on the geometric image. You can keep the grid on your crystal altar. Crystal grids are an excellent way to amplify your intentions; check out Figure 3 for inspiration!

Figure 3: An organization of crystals in a flower of life grid, including rose quartz at the center and a sage smudge stick for crystal cleansing.

- **Crystals for your car:** Your car is a great place for crystals. Place tiger's eye and clear quartz under the driver's seat for protection and clarity. Hang a pendulum of selenite from your rearview mirror for divine guidance on your travels.

- **Gifting crystals:** A crystal makes the perfect, thoughtful gift for anyone in your life, and better still if the stone comes from your own personal collection. When you pass along a crystal to a loved one, you are helping to spread powerful healing energy—which, in my opinion, is worth a lot more than a Starbucks gift card. Consider asking the other person to pass the crystal on again to someone else who needs it, once it has worked its healing magic on the intended.

- **Crystal-charged water:** Some practitioners like to place stones in a jar of water and set them out under the sun or moon to "charge" the water with the crystal's energy. Afterwards, you can drink the water, use it to make tea, or water your plants with it. Quartz is a popular crystal for making charged water, but my secret recipe is moonstone water charged under a new moon. Drink this water to relieve premenstrual systems or treat reproductive diseases. This recipe was powerfully healing for my postnatal pain and bleeding.

Cleansing and Charging Your Crystals

Most (though not all) crystals act as a sort of energetic "two-way street," imparting their healing energies on us and our environments while simultaneously removing our own unwanted energies. Think about it: if you use black tourmaline to remove negativity, where does that negative energy go? It cannot simply vanish; in accordance with the laws of thermodynamics, that energy still exists. Your tourmaline has absorbed it.

Additionally, crystals go through quite a long, involved, and unseen-to-you process between being mined and being added to your collection. Your stones may pass through many environments and many hands, from which they can pick up on unwanted energies.

A crystal's absorption of energies from either yourself or others can lower or negate its effectiveness in your healing work. Fortunately, there is an easy way to solve this and bring your crystals back to their full power: cleansing and charging them. There are many ways to accomplish this, and all of them are simple processes. You can choose a cleansing method based on what you have available to you. Try a few and see which you personally prefer.

- **Smoke:** Cleansing with the smoke of dried herbs is a common practice across many spiritual disciplines. White sage is a popular choice, but your favorite incense will work, too. Palo santo, cedar, juniper, lavender—all are effective. You can light a bay leaf from your spice cabinet! Simply light your incense, get the smoke flowing, and let your crystals bathe in it (see Figure 4). Visualize the unwanted energies being carried away with the smoke as it dissipates.
- **Running water:** Water itself is a powerful spiritual healer. While a natural source is best, such as a bubbling stream, you can use your tap water, too. The key is that the water moves over the crystal, rinsing away its unwanted energies so that its own vibrations can shine forth.
- **Sunlight:** The powerful energy of the sun can cleanse away unwanted energies, much the same as you feel your own spirits brighten on a sunny day versus a cloudy one. You can leave crystals in direct sunlight to charge them, preferably placed directly on the Earth—but be careful not to leave them out for longer than about eight hours. Some crystals are sensitive to direct sunlight, and their colors may fade if left unattended too long.
- **With another crystal:** Yes, you can cleanse a crystal with another crystal! You can charge a crystal with another to imbue some of its energy. Selenite is the top choice for this, as it is one of the very few crystals that never absorbs negative energy and therefore is always at its full charge. You can purchase a selenite plate to set your crystals on or tap them with a selenite wand. You can even place your crystals in a regular bowl with a piece of selenite to cleanse them all at once.

Figure 4: A stick of palo santo incense can be used for smoke cleansing. Here, the smoke is cleansing an entire crystal collection at once.

So, how often should you cleanse and charge your crystals? A good rule of thumb is to cleanse your entire collection once every month, but in truth, it varies greatly. Crystals that are used more frequently will likely need more frequent recharging, but using a crystal once can zap its energies if you've used it for a particularly strong healing. If you're not getting the same results you'd normally expect from a favorite crystal, chances are it's time to break out your favorite charging method.

As with all things, trust your intuition when it comes to cleansing your crystals. As you work with your collection, you'll begin to sense each specimen's particular energy, which will help you recognize when something is "off."

After reading these two chapters, you are equipped with everything you need to know to confidently begin your journey to healing with crystals! Next, I'll take you through a comprehensive reference guide to over 60 of the most essential crystals, including how to recognize them, their rarity, their healing properties, and which crystals they work best (and worst!) with.

Part II
Your Complete Reference Guide to Healing Crystals

Chapter Three

Encyclopedia of Over 60 Essential Crystals: Their Properties and Healing Powers

Believe it or not, there are more than 5,400 distinct minerals currently recognized by the International Mineralogical Association, and new varieties are added every year.[4] While you won't find five thousand different stones in your local rock stop, the variety to choose from can be quite daunting even at a *fraction* of this total!

To help you find the right crystals for your growing collection, I've compiled an encyclopedia of more than 60 of the most essential healing stones, organized by color. In these tables, you'll find the stone's pronunciation, its rarity (expressed as expense), descriptions of its common colors and shapes, the chakra with which the stone is connected—more on that in Chapter 5—and a detailed list of its healing properties in the physical, mental, and spiritual realms, including which crystals work best in combination to produce your desired effects. You may discover some interesting historical and mineralogical facts along the way.

I've said it before, and I'll say it again: when choosing your stones, *rely on your intuition*. This encyclopedia is meant to be a guide, not a set of hard-and-fast rules. As you grow more comfortable with your crystal healing practice, you'll start to experiment and find your own uses and pairings for the stones listed here. That journal I told you to keep in Chapter 2 will come in handy again; write down your observations, what works for you and what doesn't. (Or use the journal pages in the back of this book.) Over time, a whole new world of intuitive crystal healing will open to you!

Clear Quartz (kwawrts)

Rarity	$
Color	Colorless, sometimes translucent white
Structure & Shape	Hexagonal; distinct six-sided prism ending in a six-sided pyramid
Chakra	Crown

Healing Properties

Physical	Powerfully stimulating to the immune system; cleanses and detoxifies all organs
Mental	Enhances concentration, promotes clarity, and unlocks hidden memories
Spiritual	Sucks up negative energy like a vacuum cleaner; harmonizes all chakras; cleanses the soul; promotes intuition and psychic abilities; brings the body, mind, and spirit into alignment

The "master healer," Quartz is the most abundant mineral in the Earth's crust. Clear quartz is made of pure SiO_2 and is the "parent crystal" to many varieties of healing stones on this list. It has an extremely high, steady vibrational frequency.

Pair With	Literally any stone to amplify its properties

Herkimer Diamond (hur-*kuh*-mer **dahy**-m*uh*nd)

Rarity	**$$$$**	
Color	Colorless to cloudy, translucent cream	
Structure & Shape	Hexagonal; double-terminated prisms	
Chakra	Crown; Third Eye	
Healing Properties		
Physical	Excellent choice for pain relief; detoxifying; boosts the immune response; prevents physical exhaustion; heals the eyes and improves eyesight	
Mental	Aids in self-acceptance; clears away subconscious fears; relaxing	
Spiritual	Manifests pure spiritual light; clears and activates the aura; calls divine light to facilitate healing	

Herkimer diamonds are not diamonds at all but rare double-terminated clear quartz crystals found only in a single New York deposit. As such, Herkimer diamonds amplify the high vibrations of clear quartz and are great for bi-directional energy transfer. It is known as an attunement stone for this reason.

Pair With	Moldavite for powerful spiritual growth, starting a "new life;" mangano calcite to heal both physical and emotional pains; tiger's eye for powerful eye healing

Selenite (sel-*uh*-nahyt)

Rarity	**$**$$$$
Color	Translucent white to colorless
Structure & Shape	Monoclinic; forms in tabular, prismatic, or columnar crystals; commonly carved into a variety of shapes
Chakra	Crown; Third Eye

Healing Properties

Physical	Aligns the spinal column and repairs skeletal deformities; treats epilepsy; reverses the effects of free radicals on the body's cells
Mental	Clears the monkey mind; brings insight and assists in decision making
Spiritual	Assists in meditation; excellent for past life work as well as divining the future

Selenite is a crystalline form of the mineral gypsum. It is especially soft and flaky for a stone. Selenite is one of the rare crystals that never needs cleansing or charging; its energies are always right where you need them. In fact, you can use selenite to cleanse your *other* crystals!

Pair With	Black tourmaline to absorb all negativity and light the way for your highest path; moldavite when you need to make a big, positive change in your life; azurite for back pain and spinal health

Howlite (**hou**-lahyt)

Rarity	$$
Color	White with gray or black marbling
Structure & Shape	Monoclinic; typically microcrystalline and often purchased tumbled
Chakra	Crown; Root

Healing Properties

Physical	Balances calcium levels in the body; great for teeth and bones; treats osteoporosis
Mental	Treats insomnia; calms anger; promotes memory and clear communication
Spiritual	Can help develop patience; facilitates spiritual awareness; promotes creativity

Howlite is a borate mineral often mined in Canada. It has a strong connection to the mind and is known as the stone of awareness—an excellent choice for meditation. This white stone is sometimes found dyed.

Pair With	Rose quartz to let go of rage or heal anger issues; amethyst for sleep; chrysocolla for creative self-expression

Apophyllite (*uh*-**pof**-*uh*-lahyt)

Rarity	**$$**
Color	Most commonly a creamy clear or white color; many other colors possible, including green and pink
Structure & Shape	Tetragonal; forms in dipyramidal prisms, typically found in geode clusters as druzy stones
Chakra	Third Eye; Heart
Healing Properties	
Physical	Treats breathing troubles, such as asthma and seasonal allergies
Mental	Improves memory; releases us from fear; banishes negative energy
Spiritual	A stone of enlightenment; connects your heart to your higher purpose; highly cleansing

Apophyllite is quite soft for a crystal and has a tendency to flake easily like snow. This crystal has an especially high vibrational frequency, making it quite powerful for healing and cleansing.

Pair With	Bloodstone for making a morally difficult choice; selenite to shoot you straight into the spirit realm; malachite for asthma symptoms

White Opal (oh-p*uh*l)

Rarity	**$$$**$$
Color	Translucent to opaque white with characteristic opalescent shimmer
Structure & Shape	Amorphous by nature; often botryoidal in formation
Chakra	Crown

Healing Properties

Physical	Helps the body clear infection; lowers fever; strengthens eyesight
Mental	Intensifies emotions and helps you tap into them; strengthens will to live; stimulates creativity
Spiritual	Encourages independence; enhances spiritual consciousness

Opal is an amorphous mineral composed of SiO_2. It is found in a wide variety of colors, each of which exhibits opalescence, a striking rainbow iridescence named after this stone. White opal is perhaps the most common variety.

Pair With	Black opal for manifestation; garnet to bring passion back into a romance; angelite when battling an infection

Moonstone (**moon**-stohn)

Rarity	$$
Color	Translucent pearly blue-white to pale cream with striking opalescence
Structure & Shape	Monoclinic; prismatic, but tumbled specimens are more common than prisms
Chakra	Third Eye; Solar Plexus
Healing Properties	
Physical	Balances hormones—excellent for fertility and female reproductive health in general; aids digestion; reduces swelling
Mental	Promotes inner strength and emotional growth; soothes the mind and emotions
Spiritual	Brings inspiration; enhances intuition; helps you rediscover your true self

Sometimes called hecatolite, moonstone is a gorgeous variety of feldspar named for its moonlit-like opalescence. It is known as a stone of new beginnings and is strongly tied to the divine feminine. It can occur in a variety of colors with white being the most common.

Pair With	Amethyst for sleep and dreams; sunstone for balance and spiritual guidance in all things; rose quartz for self-love

Garnet (gahr-nit)

Rarity	**$$$$**
Color	Deep brownish-red
Structure & Shape	Isometric; often found in distinct dodecahedrons (twelve-faced crystals)
Chakra	Root

Healing Properties

Physical	Powerfully invigorating and regenerative; stimulates metabolism; balances sex drive in either direction
Mental	Removes inhibitions; sharpens perception; energizes mind
Spiritual	Represents the primordial fire; promotes love and passion; can aid in recalling past lives

"Garnet" is actually the name for a *group* of silicate minerals that come in a variety of colors, but red is the most commonly seen. This semi-precious stone has been prized for its use in jewelry for millennia.

Pair With	Red jasper for a powerful root chakra activator; opal to spice things up in the bedroom; hematite for taking a test

Red Jasper (jas-per)

Rarity	$~~$$$$~~
Color	Brownish, orangish red, often with black or brown banding; opaque
Structure & Shape	Hexagonal; microcrystalline by nature, often found tumbled
Chakra	Root

Healing Properties

Physical	Increases energy and stamina; prevents illness by encouraging the body's strength; promotes blood circulation; relieves diarrhea
Mental	Known as the stone of endurance, red jasper will help you get through any tribulation with force of will
Spiritual	All about balance, red jasper is both energizing and grounding

Jasper is a cryptocrystalline variety of quartz combined with other minerals, which give jasper varieties their wide range of possible colors. Red is the most common color for jasper. The color comes from iron inclusions in the crystal lattice.

Pair With	Smoky quartz to overcome a creative block; black tourmaline for grounding, amethyst for full mind and body protection against negative energies

Fire Agate (ag-it)

Rarity	**$$$**$$
Color	Bands of red, from dark crimson to bright orange-red
Structure & Shape	Hexagonal; only microcrystalline and typically purchased as tumbled stones
Chakra	Sacral; Root

Healing Properties

Physical	Used to treat stomach and circulatory problems; boosts libido
Mental	Assists with cravings such as for unhealthy foods and banishes self-destructive behavior
Spiritual	Instills courage and fortitude; protective and grounding

Agate is a part of the quartz family and a type of chalcedony recognizable for its beautiful color banding, typically with white and translucent inclusions. Fire agate is one of the more expensive varieties, highly sought for its flame-like colors.

Pair With	Amethyst when you need to make a difficult decision; rose quartz to light the, *eh-hem*, fire in your relationship; obsidian to cleanse your aura

Wulfenite (**wool**-*fuh*-nahyt)

Wulfenite is a beautifully colored lead-containing mineral recognizable for its very thin, tabular crystal habit. While not uncommon in nature, specimens that are large and sturdy enough for jewelry are quite rare and expensive. Due to the presence of lead, you must be especially cautious with this mineral and not make charged water from it.

Rarity	**$$$**
Color	Translucent, fiery red-orange
Structure & Shape	Tetragonal; forms in thin, tabular crystals often clumped together
Chakra	Sacral

Healing Properties	
Physical	Regulates the menstrual cycle; balances the metabolism in either direction; encourages appetite
Mental	Imparts creative inspiration; encourages perseverance and determination; aids in self-awareness and introspection
Spiritual	Often used to enhance meditation; excellent for past-life work; helps one accept that life is not fair and make peace with that fact

Pair With	Amber to let go of feelings of cynicism and hopelessness; hematite to bring on a late menstrual period; peridot to take life into your own hands

Vanadinite (*vuh*-**nad**-n-ahyt)

Rarity	**$$$$**
Color	Translucent red, from orange-red to red-brown
Structure & Shape	Hexagonal; typically forms in clusters of short, hexagonal prisms
Chakra	Root

Healing Properties	
Physical	Encourages absorption of iron; regulates hormones; highly physically energizing—relieves chronic fatigue; treats respiratory illnesses
Mental	Encourages flow of creative ideas; helps you express your inner power; aids in focus and productivity; banishes procrastination
Spiritual	Centers and grounds the soul into the physical body; aids in manifestation

Vanadinite is a type of apatite that contains lead; therefore, you must be especially cautious with this mineral. It should not be used to make charged water, as the result could be poisonous. It is dense and brittle, making it difficult to work with, and relatively rare.

Pair With	Orange calcite to overcome a creative block; pyrite for the perfect combo of grounding and energizing; lepidolite for relief from menopausal symptoms

Carnelian (kahr-**neel**-y*uh*n)

Rarity	**$**$$$$
Color	Translucent red-orange, ranging from muted and brownish to fiery-bright, often with white banding
Structure & Shape	Trigonal, but microcrystalline by nature; usually found tumbled
Chakra	Sacral; Root

Carnelian is a fiery variety of chalcedony. Ancient Egyptian master architects wore carnelian to mark their skill and rank. The word "carnelian" comes from the Latin for "flesh."

Healing Properties

Physical	Stimulates the sex organs; treats depression; heals kidneys and lower back pain; promotes nutrient absorption
Mental	Excellent for overcoming any kind of past abuse or healing your inner child; promotes career success
Spiritual	Promotes positive life choices and helps you stay focused on your goals; warm and comforting

Pair With	Tiger's eye to both ground and energize; garnet to balance energies in your sexual relationships; amazonite for back pain and injuries

Sunstone (**suhn**-stohn)

Rarity	$$$
Color	Blooming with shimmery coral, shades of orange and red
Structure & Shape	Triclinic; prismatic crystals are very rare
Chakra	Sacral

Healing Properties

Physical	Treats ulcers; relieves stomach pain and nausea; heals the spine
Mental	Dissipates fear and stress; encourages independence; antidepressant properties, instills optimism
Spiritual	Brings good luck and prosperity; lets your true self shine through

Sunstone is a feldspar mineral that positively blooms with sunny colors. As prismatic crystals, sunstone is a rare, prized coral-colored gem, but tumbled microcrystalline stones are easy enough to procure.

Pair With	Moonstone to harmonize yin and yang; pyrite to guard against manipulation and protect against undue criticism; citrine for stomach trouble

Amber (am-ber)

Rarity	**$$**	
Color	Translucent; various shades of gold, orange or yellow	
Structure & Shape	Amorphous solid	
Chakra	Solar Plexus; Sacral	
Healing Properties		
Physical	Revitalizes tissues, especially in the brain; treats respiratory problems; soothes chronic pain; heals kidneys, bladder, and gallbladder	
Mental	Swaps negative thoughts for positive ones; quiets the inner critic; encourages a sense of empowerment; treats depression	
Spiritual	Purifying and rejuvenating; imparts spiritual balance and stability; channels warmth	

Amber is not a mineral at all but fossilized pine tree resin that has crystalized. Specimens range in cost greatly based on their clarity and inclusions (or lack there-of). Some amber specimens have preserved organisms inside!

Pair With	Sunstone to help you be a more patient and compassionate partner in love; carnelian to relieve urinary troubles; hematite for recovering from a brain injury

Golden Topaz (toh-paz)

Rarity	$$$
Color	Ranging from yellow to orange to a warm, tawny brown
Structure & Shape	Orthorhombic; forms commonly in perfect prismatic crystals
Chakra	Solar Plexus; Sacral
Healing Properties	
Physical	Heals liver and gallbladder; regenerates cells; aids digestion; treats eating disorders
Mental	Encourages optimism; imparts a drive toward success
Spiritual	Strengthens faith; brings joy and generosity; promotes honesty with the self and others

Topaz is a silicate mineral that contains aluminum. Pure topaz is colorless, but impurities impart a warm glow on golden topaz. It is a semi-precious stone often used in jewelry.

Pair With	Amethyst for recovery from alcoholism; green fluorite for anorexia or bulimia; citrine for an extra dose of get-up-and-go

Pyrite (**pahy**-rahyt)

Rarity	$
Color	Brassy, metallic gold; opaque
Structure & Shape	Cubic; forms in crystal cubes; often microcrystalline or found as fossils
Chakra	Solar Plexus

Healing Properties

Physical	Encourages cell regrowth; treats lung disorders, especially bronchitis; protects against infectious disease transmission; treats bowel incontinence
Mental	Enhances memory; stimulates intellect and encourages a deeper understanding; quiets self-critique
Spiritual	Shields against negative vibes; excellent for meditation and divination; attracts wealth

Known as "fool's gold" because it looks like gold to the untrained eye, pyrite is a common iron-bearing mineral. It forms in characteristic cubes, making pyrite a distinctive crystal in your collection.

Pair With	Citrine to manifest your dreams; jade for abundance; moss agate for pneumonia

Orange Calcite (kal-sahyt)

	Rarity	**$**$$$
	Color	Ranging from pale, tawny gold to intense yellow-orange; semi-opaque
	Structure & Shape	Trigonal; forms in rhombohedrons, but often found in geodes and fossils, as well
	Chakra	Sacral
	Healing Properties	
	Physical	Heals damaged tissue throughout the body; high physically energizing; great for the reproductive system
	Mental	Enhances creativity; helps with motivation; aids in resiliency and the plasticity of the brain
	Spiritual	Cleanses, banishes negativity, and fuels your spiritual energy
Pair With		Amazonite to quiet an upset stomach; pyrite for reproductive health; carnelian to amp up your creative powers

Calcite is a carbonate mineral and the principal component of limestone. It is highly reactive to acid, and most calcite crystals fluoresce under ultraviolet light. A common mineral, calcite often forms during the fossilization of sea creatures, creating interesting specimens such as calcite clams.

Citrine (si-treen)

Rarity	**$$$$**
Color	Translucent, warm yellow, ranging from pastel yellow to the color of a school bus
Structure & Shape	Hexagonal; distinct six-sided prism ending in a six-sided pyramid; commonly found in clusters and geodes
Chakra	Solar Plexus; Sacral

Healing Properties

Physical	Treats degenerative diseases; heals kidneys, bladder, and diabetes; stimulates digestion; resolves chemical imbalances
Mental	Raises self-esteem and fights depression, anxiety, and phobias; stimulates the intellect and creativity; improves concentration
Spiritual	Attracts wealth and prosperity; inspires feelings of joy and delight

Citrine is a golden variety of quartz crystal. Most citrine available on the market is actually heat-treated amethyst—the iron in the stone reacts and changes its color from purple to yellow. Genuine natural citrine will be more expensive to acquire, but it's incredible healing powers make it well worth the investment. Sometimes found together with amethyst in a stone called ametrine.

Pair With	Quartz for battling any long-term degenerative illness; smoky quartz for overcoming spiritual blockages; amethyst for bridging the mind and body and treating mental and mood disorders

Peridot (per-i-doh)

Rarity	**$$$$**
Color	Pale olive to bright lime green and translucent
Structure & Shape	Orthorhombic; forms in short, compact prisms
Chakra	Heart

Healing Properties

Physical	Strengthens immune system; boosts metabolism; good for the skin; treats ulcers
Mental	Alleviates jealousy, bitterness, and resentment; enhances confidence and helps you to take charge; highly motivating, banishes lethargy
Spiritual	Releases negative energies and clears your emotional space as well as the environment; brings renewal and growth

Sometimes called chrysolite, peridot is the name given to gem-quality olivine, the dark green mineral that makes up much of the earth's mantle. While not particularly rare, specimens with high clarity are valuable for their use in jewelry, therefore on the expensive side. It is the August birthstone.

Pair With	Garnet for the confidence and drive to start a new business or career endeavor; clear quartz for powerful emotional healing; moonstone to help you recognize and overcome negative patterns

Moldavite (**mohl**-d*uh*-vahyt)

	Rarity	**$$$$$**
	Color	Translucent olive or forest green
	Structure & Shape	As a glass, moldavite does not have a crystal system; it is amorphous by nature, like obsidian (volcanic glass)
	Chakra	Third Eye; Heart
	Healing Properties	
	Physical	Aids in diagnosing illness by illuminating the problem areas; highly physically rejuvenating, encourages cells to regenerate perfectly; slows aging
	Mental	Helps you let go of the past and negative patterns in your life; encourages deep introspection, which can be painful and difficult emotionally—but it's worth the work!
	Spiritual	Connected to the stars, moldavite is a powerful conduit to the divine; excellent for meditation and scrying; encourages you to ascend to new spiritual heights

Moldavite is a much debated crystal in healing circles due to its *very* high vibrational frequency. It is actually a type of glass created by a meteorite impact on earth (called a tektite). It is found only in Czechoslovakia, it is quite rare and expensive. It has been utilized as a spiritual stone since ancient times—moldavite was discovered alongside the Venus of Willendorf![5] It is known as the stone of transformation.

Pair With	Rose quartz to carry you through difficult times with love; garnet to attract passionate love; black tourmaline to add protective energy to moldavite's transformative energy

Unakite (**yoo**-ni-kahyt)

Rarity	$$$$$	
Color	Various shades of olive green mottled with pink/coral	
Structure & Shape	Monoclinic; cryptocrystalline by nature and popular as tumbled stones	
Chakra	Third Eye; Heart	
Healing Properties		
Physical	Aids in recovery from any severe illness; encourages a healthy pregnancy and birth; encourages weight gain where needed; stimulates hair growth	
Mental	Balances emotions; aids in overcoming psychological blocks	
Spiritual	Encourages spiritual rebirth by gently releasing blockages	

Unakite is actually a type of granite rock composed of feldspar (the pink segments) and epidote (the green). This high-vibrational healing stone represents rebirth. It is sometimes called unakite jasper, but this name is a misnomer.

Pair With	Angelite for spiritual and psychic development; any other high-vibrational crystal, such as clear quartz, moldavite, or Herkimer diamond; golden topaz for recovery from poor nutrition, such as with anorexia

Watermelon Tourmaline (waw-ter-mel-*uh*n *toor*-m*uh*-leen)

Rarity	$$$$
Color	Bicolor (green and pink) or tricolor (with white in between)—like a slice of watermelon with the rind!
Structure & Shape	Trigonal; forms in long, prismatic crystals with many planes
Chakra	Heart
Healing Properties	
Physical	Boosts the immune system; calms hyperactivity; heals the physical heart
Mental	Relieves stress; lessens insecurities; heightens creativity
Spiritual	Protects from negative energy; balances yin and yang; attracts love and abundance

Tourmaline is a silicate mineral that contains the elements aluminum and boron. It's a semi-precious gemstone found in a wide array of colors. Watermelon tourmaline is a rare multicolored variety. It's named that way because it resembles the summer fruit.

Pair With	Lapis lazuli for nurturing friendships or attracting new ones; smoky quartz for grounding and protection; clear quartz for an immune system boost

Green Calcite (**kal**-sahyt)

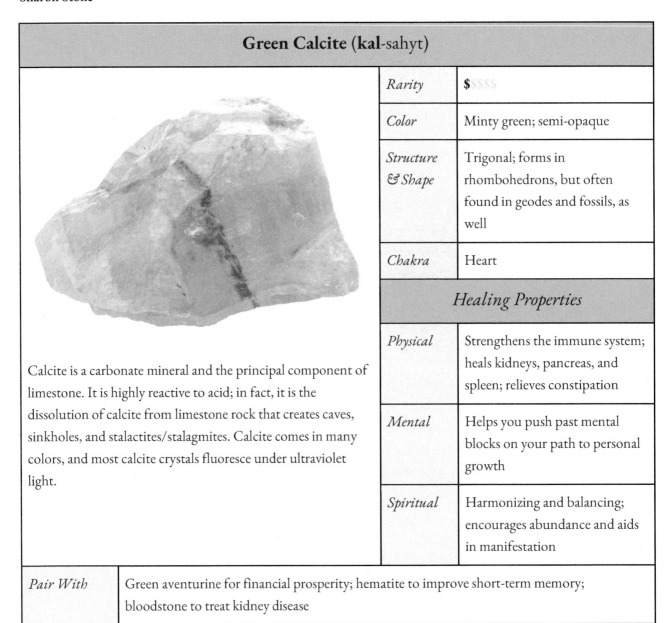

Rarity	$$$$$
Color	Minty green; semi-opaque
Structure & Shape	Trigonal; forms in rhombohedrons, but often found in geodes and fossils, as well
Chakra	Heart

Healing Properties

Physical	Strengthens the immune system; heals kidneys, pancreas, and spleen; relieves constipation
Mental	Helps you push past mental blocks on your path to personal growth
Spiritual	Harmonizing and balancing; encourages abundance and aids in manifestation

Calcite is a carbonate mineral and the principal component of limestone. It is highly reactive to acid; in fact, it is the dissolution of calcite from limestone rock that creates caves, sinkholes, and stalactites/stalagmites. Calcite comes in many colors, and most calcite crystals fluoresce under ultraviolet light.

Pair With	Green aventurine for financial prosperity; hematite to improve short-term memory; bloodstone to treat kidney disease

Chrysoprase (kris-*uh*-preyz)

Sometimes referred to as Australian jade, chrysoprase is a green chalcedony that contains the element nickel. In Ancient times, it was called the "Stone of Venus," and it was Alexander the Great's favorite gemstone.[6]

Rarity	**$$$$**
Color	Intense, opaque bright green with marblings of cream and white
Structure & Shape	Hexagonal; cryptocrystalline by nature
Chakra	Heart; Solar Plexus
Healing Properties	
Physical	Flushes toxins from the body; balances hormones; soothes digestive system; promotes restful sleep
Mental	Promotes personal strength and tenacity; boosts willpower; heals the inner child
Spiritual	Balances yin and yang; spiritually recharging; represents security and trust
Pair With	Rose quartz after a break up, when you're ready to move on; fuchsite to conquer career-related challenges; jade for a total mind and body detox

Jade (jeyd)

Rarity		$$$$$
Color		So green, they named a color after it. Ranges from deep leafy green to pale gray-green.
Structure & Shape		Monoclinic; microcrystalline—prismatic crystals are exceedingly rare
Chakra		Heart
Healing Properties		
Physical		Flushes out the body—perfect for kidneys and adrenal glands; detoxifies, great for clear skin; promotes fertility
Mental		Releases negative thoughts; encourages dreams; help you let go of emotions and find inner calm
Spiritual		Attracts good luck and love; symbolizes serenity

Jade actually refers to two different minerals: both jadeite and nephrite. Famous for its prominence in East Asian art and jewelry, this green stone is highly recognizable. It also holds a special place in ancient Mesoamerican cultures.

Pair With	Carnelian for luck in business and money; clear quartz for recovering from sickness; rose quartz to bring your inner beauty to the surface

Green Aventurine (*uh*-**ven**-ch*uh*-reen)

Rarity	**$$**
Color	Ranges from deep emerald green to a soft grass green; aventurine can also be found in other colors, including blue and yellow
Structure & Shape	Hexagonal; microcrystalline, typically bought as polished stones
Chakra	Heart

Healing Properties	
Physical	Anti-inflammatory; protects the body against environmental pollutants; relaxes the nervous system; lowers cholesterol
Mental	Stabilizes the "monkey mind;" heals a cold heart
Spiritual	Encourages prosperity; channels empathy and compassion

Aventurine is a form of microcrystalline quartz that takes on a deep green hue. It has a characteristic sparkle and shimmer thanks to the inclusion of tiny bits of mica mineral.

Pair With	Rose quartz to release emotional baggage; clear quartz to prevent cancerous growth; boulder opal to super-charge your emotions and overcome ennui or anhedonia—careful, though, as this combo can *really* make you feel awakened!

Fuchsite (fyook-sahyt)		
	Rarity	$$$
	Color	Pale to emerald green, sometimes with ruby inclusions
	Structure & Shape	Monoclinic; forms in flat, flaky layers, like mica
	Chakra	Heart
	Healing Properties	
	Physical	Perfect for any kind of physical recovery—relieves pain and encourages physical regeneration and recuperation; boosts immune system
	Mental	Heals emotional wounds and promotes inner peace; encourages resilience
	Spiritual	Brings rejuvenation and renewal; encourages youthful energy
Pair With	Herkimer diamond for boosting brain waves; lepidolite for trouble in your relationship; pretty much any other crystal, as fuchsite has a very relaxed energy	

Sparkling fuchsite is a rarer green version of the common mineral muscovite. It gets its emerald shade from chromium in its crystal lattice, which lends it amazing healing properties. In fact, it is known by some as the stone of health.

Malachite (**mal**-*uh*-kahyt)

This stunning mineral is formed through chemical precipitation, causing its characteristic banding. Malachite owes its emerald color to the presence of copper in its crystal lattice.

Rarity	**$$$**
Color	Opaque and lustrous; shades of rich emerald green in characteristic concentric bands
Structure & Shape	Monoclinic; most often botryoidal in formation
Chakra	Heart
Healing Properties	
Physical	Boosts immune system; use for any type of cancer, especially with chemotherapy; great for PMS and menstrual cramps
Mental	Releases inhibitions and encourages one to embrace change; treats dyslexia
Spiritual	Powerful heart chakra opener; protective; stimulates dreams

Pair With	Green aventurine to attract money; black tourmaline for protection from negative energies; clear quartz for any type of cancer

Moss Agate (ag-it)

Rarity		**$$**$$$
Color		Shades of green banded with white, brown, or other earthy colors
Structure & Shape		Hexagonal; only microcrystalline and typically purchased as tumbled stones
Chakra		Heart
Healing Properties		
Physical		Boosts immune system and speeds recovery; targets the lungs; great for cold or flu; anti-inflammatory.
Mental		Balances the emotions, quells fear and stress, and fights depression
Spiritual		Attracts abundance and prosperity; represents new beginnings and fresh ideas

Agate is a part of the quartz family and a type of chalcedony recognizable for its beautiful color banding, typically with white and translucent inclusions. Moss agate is a gorgeously green stone that calls to mind a tranquil, mossy forest.

Pair With	Black tourmaline for a breakup, citrine for creative abundance; bloodstone for a killer cold kicker

Green Fluorite (**floor**-ahyt)

Rarity	$$
Color	Transparent green, varying from blue-green to yellow-green
Structure & Shape	Cubic; forms in characteristic cubes, but cleaves into a double four-sided pyramid
Chakra	Heart
Healing Properties	
Physical	Detoxifies the body and the air; soothes heartburn and other digestive problems; reduces swelling and inflammation
Mental	Highly mentally stimulating; aids in the treatment of eating disorders; promotes creativity and innovation
Spiritual	Expands consciousness from the heart; symbolizes growth

Fluorite is a remarkable crystal that glows under ultraviolet light thanks to trace elements in its crystal lattice. The term for this glow, "fluorescence," was actually coined after the crystal—not the other way around! Fluorite comes in a wide variety of semi-transparent colors but is most typically purple or green.

Pair With	Green calcite when you need to bring your creative A-game; mangano calcite for heart disease; purple fluorite to bring your heart and head in line with each other

Bloodstone (**bluhd**-stohn)

Rarity	**$$$**$$	
Color	Dark bluish-green speckled with characteristic blood-red flakes	
Structure & Shape	Hexagonal; inherently microcrystalline	
Chakra	Heart; Root	
Healing Properties		
Physical	Great for blood disorders or anemia; detoxifies organs, especially the liver	
Mental	Helps you adapt to unexpected changes and navigate challenging situations in life	
Spiritual	Grounding; encourages selflessness and living in the present moment	

Also known as heliotrope, bloodstone is a type of chalcedony (like agate) that contains flecks of red hematite. It's very recognizable for this distinct color combination.

Pair With	Chrysoprase for emotional balance and stability; turquoise for aid with absorbing the nutrients in foods; clear quartz after significant blood loss, such as a heavy menstrual cycle

Amazonite (am-*uh*-*zuh*-nahyt)

Rarity	$$$
Color	Light to bright blue-green with white or cream-colored veining
Structure & Shape	Triclinic; found in microcrystalline form as polished stones
Chakra	Heart; Throat
Healing Properties	
Physical	Great for calcium-deficiency or tooth/bone decay; relieves muscle spasms
Mental	Powerful brain booster; soothes worry and dispels negative energies; maintains emotional bonds
Spiritual	Balances masculine and feminine energies; helps you see both sides of a problem

Amazonite, sometimes called "Amazon stone," is a variety of feldspar, which is actually very common in the Earth's crust—but this particular type of blue-green feldspar is comparatively rare.

Pair With	Green aventurine for making sound financial moves; moldavite if you're going gambling; blue lace agate for a broken bone

Chrysocolla (kris-*uh*-kol-*uh*)

Rarity	$$$
Color	Bright green-blue and opaque, often with brown inclusions
Structure & Shape	Orthorhombic; usually botryoidal, meaning many clumps of rounded segments
Chakra	Throat; Heart
Healing Properties	
Physical	Detoxifies liver and kidneys; good for bones and blood; strengthens muscles and relieves cramps (including menstrual)
Mental	Helps relieve guilt and ease heartache; encourages self-awareness; treats phobias
Spiritual	Re-energizes all chakras and brings joy into your soul; promotes creativity

Chrysocolla is an eye-catching stone that may be confused with turquoise. Like azurite and malachite, it owes its color to the presence of copper in its crystal lattice. It has long been used for healing in African and Native American cultures.

Pair With	Amethyst for alcoholism and substance abuse recovery; citrine for stomach cramps; smoky quartz if you're ready to take a good, hard look at yourself—it's worth it!

Turquoise (**tur**-koiz)

Rarity	**$$**
Color	Opaque; an unmistakable shade of greenish blue with cream or brown
Structure & Shape	Triclinic; cryptocrystalline and amorphous by nature
Chakra	Throat

Healing Properties

Physical	Helps the body absorb nutrients; encourages tissue regeneration; purifies the lungs; treats cataracts
Mental	Induces calm, especially in chaotic situations; prevents panic attacks; helps you articulate your thoughts
Spiritual	Highly purifying; promotes self-realization; reveals the truth and spiritual wisdom

Turquoise is one of the oldest stones to be mined and used by humans. It owes its characteristic blue shade (for which the color is named) to the copper in its crystal lattice.

Pair With	Aquamarine for powerful throat chakra healing; moonstone to guide and protect you on a journey; malachite to shield yourself from outside influences

Blue Apatite (ap-*uh*-tahyt)

Rarity	**$$**$$$
Color	Ranging from vibrant blue to sea-green with marbling (commonly gold or brown)
Structure & Shape	Hexagonal; often microcrystalline or found in six-sided prisms
Chakra	Throat

Healing Properties	
Physical	Suppresses hunger and raises metabolism; treats arthritis and joint pain; stabilizes blood pressure
Mental	Clears confusion and increases motivation; highly balancing, it can also slow down an overactive mind
Spiritual	Manifestation; balance; connects us with our inner humanitarian and promotes altruism

Apatite is a common phosphate mineral that comes in many varieties and colors, including blue, green, and yellow. Blue apatite in particular is a great healer, and in the past, it was crushed and used as pigment for its vibrant hues. This stone carries a powerful energy of manifestation.

Pair With	Lapis lazuli to meet your life's purpose and manifest your dreams; amethyst to encourage psychic and intuitive abilities; iolite to crush your weight loss goals

Aquamarine (ah-kw*uh*-m*uh*-**reen**)

Rarity	**$$$**	
Color	Translucent sky blue	
Structure & Shape	Hexagonal; typically prisms with a flat top; large, whole crystals are common	
Chakra	Throat	

Healing Properties

Physical	Treats thyroid problems; regulates hormones; relieves swelling, especially good for a sore throat; prevents miscarriage
Mental	Helps you overcome judgemental attitudes and encourages tolerance; sharpens the intellect; promotes inner peace
Spiritual	Brings closure; taps into your intuition; protects your aura

Aquamarine is a blue variety of beryl. It is a semi-precious gemstone often used in jewelry and the birthstone for those born in the month of March.

Pair With	Rhodonite if you need some help opening your heart; moonstone for a healthy pregnancy; blue calcite to improve communication with difficult people

Blue Topaz (toh-paz)

Rarity	$$$
Color	Translucent, ranging from deep blue to sky blue
Structure & Shape	Orthorhombic; forms commonly in perfect prismatic crystals
Chakra	Throat
Healing Properties	
Physical	Relieves migraines; eases jaw tension; encourages overall body wellness
Mental	Imparts wisdom; aids in uncovering the truth; helps you communicate clearly
Spiritual	Helps you find your path if you've lost sight of your personal truth; brings body, mind, and spirit into alignment

Topaz is a silicate mineral that contains aluminum. Pure topaz is colorless, but impurities give blue topaz a stunning sky-blue hue. It is a semi-precious stone often used in jewelry and the birthstone of December.

Pair With	Kunzite for migraines; labradorite for some heavy-duty soul searching; golden topaz to help you keep the faith

Blue Kyanite (kahy-*uh*-nahyt)

Rarity	**$$**	
Color	Opaque blue, ranging from deep to pale	
Structure & Shape	Triclinic; forms in long, thin crystals flattened like the blade of a knife	
Chakra	Throat	
Healing Properties		
Physical	Relieves pain; helps clear infections; lowers blood pressure; relaxes muscles	
Mental	Encourages self-expression; calms the mind and emotions	
Spiritual	Fosters deep connection with others; helps you enter a meditative state; excellent for most metaphysical purposes	

Blue kyanite is a silicate mineral that contains aluminum, giving the stone its blue hue. In fact, the name kyanite comes from the Greek *kuanos*, meaning blue. Kyanite is one of the rare stones that does not require energetic cleansing, as it does not take on negative energies.

Pair With	Labradorite to align all of your chakras and travel inward; selenite to clear bad vibes; black tourmaline for pain relief

Blue Lace Agate (leys **ag**-it)

Rarity	**$$**$$$
Color	Light blue with white and/or brown banding
Structure & Shape	Hexagonal; only microcrystalline and typically purchased as tumbled stones
Chakra	Throat

Healing Properties	
Physical	Treats thyroid and lymphatic problems; encourages bone repair; soothes irritated skin
Mental	Highly calming; brings tranquility and neutralizes anger
Spiritual	Helps you find your voice and speak your heart

Agate is a part of the quartz family and a type of chalcedony recognizable for its beautiful color banding, typically with white and translucent inclusions. Blue lace agate is a delicate-looking stone with ribbons of pale blue and white.

Pair With	Rose quartz if you need help talking to a loved one about a difficult topic; lapis lazuli before a public speaking event to boost your confidence

Sodalite (**sohd**-l-ahyt)

Rarity	**$$**
Color	Ranging from ultramarine to navy blue with white marbling
Structure & Shape	Cubic; very rarely forms in crystals, instead commonly microcrystalline; often purchased tumbled
Chakra	Third Eye; Throat
Healing Properties	
Physical	Prevents erratic spikes in blood sugar levels; combats radiation damage— excellent for radiation therapy patients; clears congestion; soothes sore throat and hoarse speech
Mental	Encourages rational thought and objectivity; helps verbalize feelings; perfect for preventing panic attacks
Spiritual	Enhances self-esteem; represents communication

With its deep blue color, sodalite is easily confused for lapis lazuli, but it lacks the characteristic pyrite flakes of the latter stone. Sodalite is a powerful healer of the mind and body.

Pair With	Tiger's eye for focus at work; lapis lazuli to increase mental capabilities; aquamarine if you've lost your voice

Lapis Lazuli (lap-is laz-*oo*-lee)

Lapis lazuli is a semi-precious stone that has been prized for centuries for its deep blue color. In the middle ages, it was ground into powder to make one of the most sought-after paint pigments: ultramarine.

Rarity	**$$$**$$
Color	Incredibly blue, deep and vivid, like ultramarine, with white and gold inclusions
Structure & Shape	Cubic; microcrystalline is standard
Chakra	Third-Eye; Throat
Healing Properties	
Physical	Soothes inflammation; great for throat and vocal chords; cleanses organs; treats thyroid diseases
Mental	Releases stress and brings peace to the mind; encourages mental clarity
Spiritual	Protects against psychic attacks; encourages self-awareness and objectivity
Pair With	Turquoise for cultivating forgiveness; selenite for enhanced spiritual awareness; aquamarine for thyroid imbalance

Labradorite (lab-*ruh*-daw-rahyt)

Rarity	**$$$**
Color	Multicolored, most typically blue and brown; characteristically iridescent
Structure & Shape	Triclinic; typically forms in thin, tabular crystals; often purchased tumbled
Chakra	Crown; Third Eye

Healing Properties

Physical	Treats vision and eye problems; targets the brain; regulates metabolism and hormones; great for kicking a cold
Mental	Dispels illusions to reveal the truth; quells insecurity; stimulates imagination
Spiritual	Strengthens intuition; represents transformation and helps guide one through change; protects the aura

Few crystals catch the light quite like labradorite, with its shimmery, rainbow planes of blue, green, red, orange, and yellow. This particular variety of iridescence is called "labradorescence;" it is caused by light hitting "twinning" crystal surfaces within the stone.

Pair With	Lapis lazuli for enhancing psychic abilities; hematite for healing a brain injury; blue dumortierite to enhance mental prowess

Blue Dumortierite (doo-**mawr**-tee-*uh*-rahyt)

Rarity	$$$
Color	Violet blue to blue-gray, typically dark with black banding
Structure & Shape	Orthorhombic; forms prismatic crystals but more commonly found in microcrystalline form
Chakra	Third Eye; Throat
Healing Properties	
Physical	Fantastic at treating headaches; relaxes tense muscles
Mental	Calms over-excitement and promotes verbalization of ideas—perfect for easing symptoms of ADHD and autism
Spiritual	Brings patience and calm; opens your third eye to new ways of understanding

Dumortierite is a silicate mineral that contains aluminum. It is most often violet blue, but green and red varieties also exist. It sometimes grows intermingled with quartz and called "blue dumortierite quartz," one of the rarer blue quartz varieties.

Pair With	Clear quartz for full-body healing and relaxation; any intense crystal, such as moldavite, to reign in its energies; amethyst for fighting an addiction, either chemical or emotional

Angelite (eyn-j*uh*l-ahyt)

	Rarity	**$$$$**
	Color	Soft, light blue (like a glacier)—sometimes lilac blue—to nearly white
	Structure & Shape	Orthorhombic; tabular prisms are very rare while microcrystalline forms are more common
	Chakra	Third Eye; Crown; Throat
	Healing Properties	
	Physical	Heals infections; treats the thyroid; assists weight loss; promotes heart and blood health
	Mental	Relieves tension and calms anger; helps you to forgive
	Spiritual	Powerfully spiritual; connects you to the celestial realm and your spirit guides

Angelite, also called anhydrite, is a form of gypsum, and gem quality specimens are very rare—though it's easy to get your hands on a polished stone. Angelite is in fact Selenite that has been highly compressed over many, many years.

Pair With	Hematite for treating diseases of the blood or anemia; fluorite for problem-solving; clear quartz for divine guidance

Celestite (sel-*uh*-stahyt)

Rarity	**$$**$$$
Color	Pale, transparent sky blue to periwinkle gray
Structure & Shape	Orthorhombic; can form complex pyramidal crystals, but almost always found as geodes
Chakra	Crown; Third Eye; Throat
	Healing Properties
Physical	Aids bone growth and repair; relaxes nerves; induces sleep
Mental	Emotionally soothing; aids lucid dreaming and enhances the vividness of dreams
Spiritual	This high-vibration stone encourages psychic abilities; used for astral projection; promotes mindfulness

Named for its heavenly, celestial color, celestite is a crystal commonly found in geodes. In fact, the largest known geode in the world is made of celestite. While it's not rare, the price point will vary based on the color and quality of a specimen.

Pair With	Angelite for a direct phone line to your spirit guides; amethyst to take your sleeping dreams to the next spiritual level; amazonite for a toothache

Azurite (azh-*uh*-rahyt)

Ancient cultures such as the Mayans, Egyptians, and ancient Chinese held azurite in very high regard as a spiritual conduit and a psychic stone. It often forms alongside green malachite, calling to mind the green Earth and blue seas of our planet.

Rarity	**$$$**
Color	Deep, dark azure blue—nearly indigo
Structure & Shape	Monoclinic; forms in tabular or prismatic crystals, but more commonly purchased in microcrystalline form
Chakra	Third Eye

Healing Properties	
Physical	Excellent for treating ailments of the vertebrae and aligning the spinal column; detoxifies organs and stimulates blood flow, especially to the skin
Mental	Stimulates intellect and opens the mind to new ideas and perspectives
Spiritual	Awakens the third eye and illuminates your spiritual path; encourages psychic abilities

Pair With	Malachite for full body awareness and healing, combining strength of heart with an open third eye; chrysocolla to harness divine wisdom

Purple Fluorite (**floor**-ahyt)

Rarity	**$$**$$$
Color	Transparent purple; varies from pale pinky-purple to deep indigo, but most often a royal violet
Structure & Shape	Cubic; forms in characteristic cubes, but cleaves into a double four-sided pyramid
Chakra	Third Eye
Healing Properties	
Physical	Promotes muscle relaxation, relieving physical symptoms of stress; detoxifies the body and the air; soothes nerve-related pains
Mental	Highly mentally stimulating; excellent in treating mental and mood disorders of all kinds; improves mental acuity
Spiritual	Stimulates the pineal gland to open the third eye; boosts psychic powers and intuition; can clarify your spiritual path to you

Fluorite is a remarkable crystal that glows under ultraviolet light thanks to trace elements in its crystal lattice. The term for this glow, "fluorescence," was actually coined after the crystal—not the other way around! Fluorite comes in a wide variety of semi-transparent colors but is most typically purple or green.

Pair With	Green fluorite to balance emotions with thoughts; citrine to banish depression; black tourmaline to relieve symptoms of fibromyalgia

Iolite (**ahy**-*uh*-lahyt)

Rarity	$$$
Color	Translucent purplish gray to deep indigo
Structure & Shape	Orthorhombic; often forms in twin prisms; can be commonly found tumbled
Chakra	Third Eye; Throat

Healing Properties

Physical	Detoxifies and regenerates the liver; aids in weight loss; relieves headache and fever
Mental	Treats addictions; encourages self-expression
Spiritual	Opens the third eye and invites psychic visions; encourages taking responsibility for oneself; promotes independence

Iolite is a name for gem quality Cordierite, an iron-containing mineral. Also known as "water sapphire," this pretty purple stone's colors may appear to change based on the way the light hits it.

Pair With	Peridot for financial independence; amethyst for detox and addiction; garnet to invigorate the body, heart, and intellect

Amethyst (am-*uh*-thist)

Rarity	**$$**$$$
Color	Purple; varies from a clear, deep violet to a soft lavender
Structure & Shape	Hexagonal; distinct six-sided prism ending in a six-sided pyramid; commonly found in clusters and geodes
Chakra	Crown; Third Eye
Healing Properties	
Physical	Eases pain, especially headaches; treats insomnia; balances the endocrine system; a powerful cancer fighting stone!
Mental	Encourages sobriety; induces calm and tranquility; protects against psychic attack
Spiritual	Encourages intuition and insights powerful dreams; connects you to the spiritual realm

Amethyst is a quartz crystal that has been colored purple by inclusions of different metals during crystallization. These metals replace SiO_2 molecules in the crystal lattice in intricate ways, which gives this violet crystal its remarkable healing energies.

Pair With	Rose quartz when you're entering a new romantic relationship; clear quartz if you are battling a long-term illness; citrine for manifestation

Sugilite (soo-gee-layht)

Rarity	**$$$$**
Color	Various shades of purple, from deep blue-violet to bright pinkish purple—most commonly compared to "grape jelly"
Structure & Shape	Hexagonal; prismatic crystals are exceptionally rare, usually found in microcrystalline form
Chakra	Crown; Heart
Healing Properties	
Physical	Relieves tension and tension-related pains; balances the nervous system; cleanses the lymphatic system
Mental	Clears the mind—highly recommended to ease symptoms for those on the autism spectrum; encourages deep emotional bonds with others
Spiritual	Highly nurturing; clears away attachments that are holding you back; protects empaths from soaking up others' energies; great for sleep and dreams

Rare sugilite is a beautiful pinkish purple silicate mineral. It carries a powerful love energy, similar to rose quartz, and like many pinkish stones, it owes its color to the inclusion of manganese.

Pair With	Iolite when you need to "let it go;" amethyst for ADHD symptoms; blue dumortierite for nonverbal autism

Lepidolite (li-**pid**-l-ahyt)

Rarity	$$$$
Color	Pinky purple, from lilac gray to magenta
Structure & Shape	Monoclinic; forms in tabular or prismatic crystals, but more commonly found in a flaky aggregation, like mica
Chakra	Crown; Third Eye

Healing Properties

Physical	Treats epilepsy and Alzheimer's; relaxes the nervous system; great for the spine and joints
Mental	Stabilizes mood swings; perfect for menopause; treats eating disorders
Spiritual	Eases transitions; helps guide you into the future; facilitates astral travel

Lepidolite is a lithium-containing variety of mica that is relatively rare on Earth, prized both for its rare element composition and its beauty. It is known as a "stone of transition," great to have around when you're going through a change.

Pair With	Amethyst when mourning the death of a loved one; tiger's eye for mood swings; black onyx after a seizure

Kunzite (**koonts**-ahyt)

	Rarity	$$
	Color	Transparent pink, from barbie pink to ballet slipper pink to pinky lilac
	Structure & Shape	Monoclinic; forms in prisms
	Chakra	Third Eye; Heart
	Healing Properties	
	Physical	Great for PMS and period symptoms; eases stress; treats migraines
	Mental	Helps overcome past traumas; clears emotional blockages; encourages adaptability
	Spiritual	Connected to feminine/yin energies; encourages empathy

Kunzite is a gem quality variety of the mineral spodumene. The inclusion of manganese is what gives this stone its delicate pink color, much like mangano calcite, which calls to mind matters of the heart and femininity.

Pair With	Pink tourmaline if you're a struggling mom; moonstone for women's reproductive health; lapis lazuli to help get the most out of talk therapy

Pink Tourmaline (***toor***-m*uh*-leen)

Tourmaline is a silicate mineral that contains the elements aluminum and boron. It's a semi-precious gemstone found in a wide array of colors. Also known as rubellite, pink tourmaline is a favorite for jewelry because it's crystal-clear and comes in such a wide selection of pink shades.

Rarity	**$$$**$$
Color	Ranging from pale, translucent pink to a dark pink-red
Structure & Shape	Trigonal; forms in long, prismatic crystals with many planes
Chakra	Heart

Healing Properties	
Physical	Releases tension; improves hand-eye coordination
Mental	Relaxing; attracts creative inspiration; relieves paranoia; balances right and left brain hemispheres
Spiritual	Helps you understand yourself and others; encourages compassion and tolerance

Pair With	Rhodochrosite to smooth over emotional conflicts; rose quartz to attract love into your life; blue topaz for total mind and body relaxation

Rhodonite (rohd-n-ahyt)

Rhodonite is a relatively rare mineral found in only a few deposits around the world. It owes its pink color to manganese and is powerfully associated with the heart chakra.

Rarity	**$$$**
Color	From pale pink to deep, rosy pink-red with black veining
Structure & Shape	Triclinic; forms in tabular crystals, but these are quite rare—cryptocrystalline is much more common
Chakra	Heart
Healing Properties	
Physical	Treats hearing loss; relieves itching; reduces scarring
Mental	Encourages compassion for others; helps heal from abuse; builds up confidence
Spiritual	All about love for oneself and others; powerfully emotional healing

Pair With	Rose quartz uncover emotions hidden by trauma and apathy; rhodochrosite to find oneself after a breakup; moonstone for fertility

Rhodochrosite (rohd-*uh*-**croh**-sahyt)

Rarity	**$$**$$$
Color	Various shades of pink, often banded with white
Structure & Shape	Hexagonal; very rarely forms in rhombohedral crystals, more commonly found in microcrystalline form
Chakra	Heart
	Healing Properties
Physical	Regulates heart rate; raises or lowers blood pressure as needed; stimulates circulation
Mental	Improves one's sense of self-worth; lifts depression and imparts cheer; encourages positive attitude
Spiritual	Integrates the physical energy with the spiritual; energizes the soul

Rhodochrosite gets its pretty pink from manganese. In microcrystalline form, this crystal often displays lace-like banding, lending it a childlike charm that speaks to its strong positive vibrations.

Pair With	Pink tourmaline for "getting your groove back;" rose quartz to prevent heart attack; blue lace agate to strengthen friendships

Rose Quartz (rohz kwawrts)

No stone embodies the energy of pure, unconditional love quite like rose quartz. This pink variety of quartz crystal is easy to come by and a must in any collection.

Rarity	**$**
Color	Translucent, soft pink
Structure & Shape	Hexagonal; distinct six-sided prism ending in a six-sided pyramid
Chakra	Heart
	Healing Properties
Physical	Strengthens the heart; eases chest pain; speeds up recovery times; promotes fertility
Mental	Calming and reassuring; helps ease the pain of grief; encourages self-acceptance
Spiritual	Represents universal love, for the self and others; dispels negative energy and replaces it with love and tenderness

Pair With	Carnelian when trying to conceive; malachite to encourage love and forgiveness; green aventurine for heart disease

Mangano Calcite (**mang**-*guh*-noh **kal**-sahyt)

Calcite is a carbonate mineral and the principal component of limestone. It is highly reactive to acid; in fact, it is the dissolution of calcite from limestone rock that creates caves, sinkholes, and stalactites/stalagmites. Mangano calcite fluoresces bright pink under UV light thanks to the manganese in its crystal lattice.

Rarity	**$$$**
Color	Pale, milky pink with banding
Structure & Shape	Trigonal; microcrystalline by nature and typically found as polished stones
Chakra	Crown; Heart
Healing Properties	
Physical	Lowers blood pressure; eases pain; heals the entire body system
Mental	Boosts self-confidence and self-esteem as well as compassion for others; opens the floodgates to hidden emotions
Spiritual	An important stone in Reiki, it is a deep, psychic healer that brings energy down from the crown to the heart

Pair With	Hematite to prevent nightmares; rose quartz if you're in desperate need of a dose of self-love; black tourmaline to soothe full-body aches and pains

Muscovite (**muhs**-*kuh*-vahyt)

Rarity	**$$**
Color	Most commonly light brown-gray to colorless, but also comes in many other colors; always with a mirror-like, semi-metallic luster
Structure & Shape	Monoclinic; forms in thin laminate "pages" of a "book"
Chakra	Crown; Third-Eye; Heart
	Healing Properties
Physical	Aids in recovery from stroke; treats neurological dysfunctions by supporting nerve cells; encourages muscular strength; helps with hearing loss
Mental	Helps you see your own flaws without harsh judgment; calms anger and eases tensions; stops you from responding to old emotional triggers
Spiritual	Encourages intuition; maintains the integrity of your psychic energies; helps you live in the present moment

Muscovite is a phyllosilicate mineral with a beautiful, mirror-like luster. Its unique cleavage reveals perfectly flat, thin sections, often called "books" of mica. Mica, however, refers to a *group* of minerals that also includes fuchsite and lepidolite. Muscovite is important in the formation of many types of rock.

Pair With	Aquamarine for enhanced communication and understanding with loved ones; rhodonite for hearing loss; watermelon tourmaline for healing after a stroke

Smoky Quartz (**smoh**-kee kwawrts)

This dark variety of quartz crystal can be quite stunning. Smoky quartz owes its cloudy color to free silicone particles in the crystal, caused by irradiation.

Rarity	**$$**$$$
Color	Brown-gray, cloudy and translucent, often colorless in places
Structure & Shape	Hexagonal; distinct six-sided prism ending in a six-sided pyramid
Chakra	Solar Plexus; Root
Healing Properties	
Physical	Detoxifying; treats pain in the abdomen, hips, legs, and feet as well as headaches; fortifies the nervous system—great for muscle spasms
Mental	Promotes positive thoughts; lessons suicidal ideation; relieves fear and soothes stress
Spiritual	Highly grounding; prevents nightmares and helps one realize their dreams
Pair With	Blue lace agate for a crystalline antidepressant; malachite to relieve sore and aching feet; amethyst to see your deepest desires

Boulder Opal (bohl-der oh-p*uh*l)

Rarity	$$$$
Color	Similar to black opal but surrounded by a (typically brown) host rock
Structure & Shape	Amorphous by nature; often botryoidal in formation
Chakra	Crown; Base
Healing Properties	
Physical	Great for troubles with eyesight; promotes vitality; brings inner beauty to the outside
Mental	Intensifies emotions and helps you tap into them; encourages creativity; helps maintain a positive outlook
Spiritual	Helps with past life recall; can allow you to see others' spiritual auras; a direct connection to the cosmos!

Boulder opal is a rare and highly sought-after type of opal that is found only in cracks and crevices of larger rock, typically sandstone or ironstone. It is usually impossible to remove completely from the host rock.

Pair With	Labradorite for healing eye injuries or partial blindness; garnet for past life recall; selenite to align your actions with your higher spiritual purpose

Tiger's Eye (**tahy**-gerz ahy)

Rarity	**$$**$$$
Color	Stripes of gold, black, and brown with characteristic chatoyance
Structure & Shape	Trigonal; forms only in microcrystalline aggregate
Chakra	Solar Plexus; Root

Healing Properties	
Physical	Targets the eyes and improves vision; detoxifies; relieves pain; heals bones and spinal column
Mental	Focuses the mind; balances mood swings; imparts courage and raises willpower
Spiritual	Grounding and protective; brings good luck; helps you tap into your personal power

Tiger's eye is an earthy stone that exhibits chatoyance, otherwise known as the "cat's eye effect," a beautiful, shimmery shifting of light. Tiger's eye is a metamorphic quartz mineral and was used as a protective amulet in ancient times.

Pair With	Citrine for a major confidence boost; pyrite to attract abundance; black onyx to promote self-awareness

Mookaite (**moo**-kahyt)

Rarity	**$$$**	
Color	Banded in shades of yellow, red, cream, and brown; opaque and satiny	
Structure & Shape	Hexagonal; microcrystalline by nature	
Chakra	Solar Plexus; Root	
Healing Properties		
Physical	Slows aging; strengthens immune system; promotes overall health of the body	
Mental	Promotes new ideas; assists in decision making; relieves stress; facilitates emotional growth	
Spiritual	Highly nurturing and protective; helps you achieve your best self	

Mookaite is a type of jasper (and is sometimes called "mookaite jasper"). It is only found in one mine in western Australia where it is often challenging to extract. Many specimens include microscopic plankton fossils.

Pair With	Carnelian for an innovative focus; jade to stay youthful; watermelon tourmaline to stay calm and patient in the face of stress

Shiva Lingam (shiv-uh ling-guhm)

	Rarity	**$$$**
	Color	Opaque; various shades of cream, tan, and brown
	Structure & Shape	Cryptocrystalline by nature; almost exclusively found as elongated eggs—some of these are naturally occurring, but most have been carved and polished to this shape
	Chakra	All Chakras
	Healing Properties	
	Physical	Enhances moth male and female fertility; increases libido—specifically for tantric energy; encourages physical vitality
	Mental	Balances the mind; encourages creativity and invention; will pull you out of a rut
	Spiritual	Very potent spiritual power, especially regarding creation and generation; activates kundalini energy and opens all chakras
Pair With		Moldavite for powerful (though often disruptive) transformation; clear quartz when working with kundalini energy; fire agate for a powerful boost in sex drive

Shiva lingam is a cryptocrystalline variety of quartz only found at the site of a spiritually significant river in India. The name means "sign of Shiva," a great Hindu god. Shiva lingam is cut and polished into oblong shapes, representing both egg and phallus, unifying male and female.

Dalmatian Jasper (dal-**mey**-sh*uh*n **jas**-per)

Rarity	**$**~~$$$$~~
Color	Opaque, creamy white with black and/or brown "polka dots"
Structure & Shape	Hexagonal; microcrystalline by nature, often found tumbled
Chakra	Sacral; Root
	Healing Properties
Physical	Good for circulatory and digestive systems; balances the urinary tract—great for preventing leaks; balances temperature
Mental	Promotes positive thinking; dispels fear; treats depression and anxiety
Spiritual	Protective; taps into your inner child and brings joy and playfulness; balances yin and yang energies

Jasper is a cryptocrystalline variety of quartz combined with other minerals, which give jasper varieties their wide range of possible colors. Dalmatian jasper is named for its spotted appearance, like the popular dog breed, and almost exclusively originates from Chihuahua, Mexico. The dark spots on this form of jasper are actually tiny inclusions of tourmaline!

Pair With	Lapis Lazuli to help ground spiritual knowledge into the body; moss agate for overcoming childhood emotional wounds; hematite for increased blood circulation

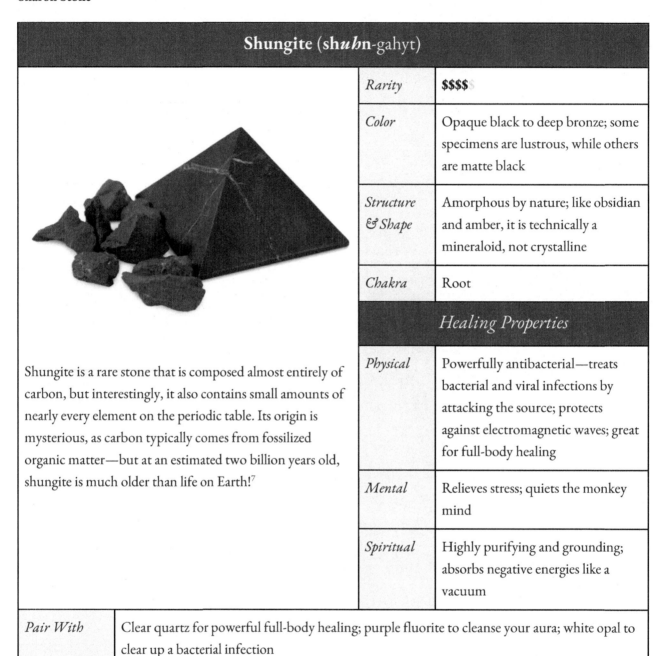

Shungite (**shuhn**-gahyt)

Rarity	**$$$$**$
Color	Opaque black to deep bronze; some specimens are lustrous, while others are matte black
Structure & Shape	Amorphous by nature; like obsidian and amber, it is technically a mineraloid, not crystalline
Chakra	Root

Healing Properties

Physical	Powerfully antibacterial—treats bacterial and viral infections by attacking the source; protects against electromagnetic waves; great for full-body healing
Mental	Relieves stress; quiets the monkey mind
Spiritual	Highly purifying and grounding; absorbs negative energies like a vacuum

Shungite is a rare stone that is composed almost entirely of carbon, but interestingly, it also contains small amounts of nearly every element on the periodic table. Its origin is mysterious, as carbon typically comes from fossilized organic matter—but at an estimated two billion years old, shungite is much older than life on Earth![7]

Pair With	Clear quartz for powerful full-body healing; purple fluorite to cleanse your aura; white opal to clear up a bacterial infection

Black Opal (oh-*puhl*)

Rarity	$$$$
Color	Dark gray to brownish black with characteristic opalescent shimmer
Structure & Shape	Amorphous by nature; often botryoidal in formation
Chakra	Root

	Healing Properties
Physical	Purifies blood; heals kidneys; boosts libido
Mental	Protects you from outside emotional influences; stops overthinking; quells fear and anxiety
Spiritual	Wards against the evil eye; protection for travelers; encourages prophetic visions

Rarer and more expensive than white opal, "black" opal is something of a misnomer. While the base color of the stone is typically dark gray or brown, that dark backdrop allows its opalescent qualities to positively explode with color!

Pair With	White opal for manifestation; fire agate for aphrodisiac properties; moonstone for a long journey

Black Tourmaline (*toor*-m*uh*-leen)

Rarity	$$\$\$$$~~\$\$\$~~
Color	Lustrous black
Structure & Shape	Trigonal; forms in long, prismatic crystals with many planes
Chakra	Root

Healing Properties

Physical	Protects the body from radiation and environmental pollution; soothes pain and encourages mobility in the legs and feet
Mental	Resolves internal conflict; dispels negative self-talk; relieves panic attacks; helps with overcoming phobias
Spiritual	Very strong protective energies; spiritually grounding; sucks up negative energies; guards against psychic attack

Tourmaline is a silicate mineral that contains the elements aluminum and boron. It's a semi-precious gemstone found in a wide array of colors, but black tourmaline is perhaps the most common. It is also known as schorl.

Pair With	Amethyst for meditation—spiritual elevation combined with earthly grounding; clear quartz to overcome negative thoughts; moldavite to temper and soften its powerful transformative energy

Hematite (hee-*muh*-tahyt)

Rarity	**$**$$$
Color	Most often shiny, metallic gray-black; sometimes metallic red-brown
Structure & Shape	Hexagonal; can appear in a variety of shapes and is often purchased tumbled
Chakra	Root

Healing Properties

Physical	Treats disorders of the blood, especially anemia; heals kidneys; promotes tissue regeneration
Mental	Enhances memory and mental focus; promotes strength of will; banishes compulsions and addictions
Spiritual	Powerfully grounding and protective; represents bravery and endurance; dissolves negative energies

This beautiful metallic crystal is known as the "stone of the mind." It has been used since ancient times to promote memory and concentration. It's high iron content gives hematite its magnetic properties as well as intense healing properties for the blood.

Pair With	Clear quartz to bring mind, body, and spirit into alignment; orange calcite if you're lacking mental motivation; tiger's eye for a one-two punch of protection and grounding

Obsidian (*uh*b-**sid**-ee-*uh*n)

Rarity	$$$$$
Color	Typically shiny black
Structure & Shape	Amorphous by nature, obsidian doesn't have a crystal system!
Chakra	Root

Healing Properties

Physical	Detoxifying; treats joint pain and arthritis; eases painful cramps
Mental	Eases tension and stress; urges intellectual exploration; clears confusion and emotional blockages
Spiritual	Protects against negativity; leads you to ultimate truths; purifies the soul

Obsidian is actually volcanic glass that forms when magma erupts and cools very quickly. This technically makes it, well, *not* a crystal, but its mineral healing properties are nonetheless strong. Though it can be found in several colors, black is by far the most common.

Pair With	Tiger's eye for major psychic protection; smoky quartz to release bad habits; carnelian to treat and prevent arthritis pain

Chapter Four

A Practical Guide to Crystal Healing Properties

"The gem cannot be polished without friction, nor human perfected without trials."
Chinese proverb

Now, you have a full encyclopedia of healing stones at your fingertips! Chapter 3 is a great resource for learning more about the crystals you may feel called to intuitively or that others have gifted to you. But I'm sure you are looking to invite *specific* healing properties into your life, and there is a better way to find the right crystal for you than reading through the encyclopedia.

Here, I've organized my recommendations for the top three healing crystals to alleviate a variety of conditions and guide you through different challenges in life. You can use this guide to quickly find crystals that correspond to your individual needs.

The Big Six

These six illnesses are the most common natural causes of death in the United States, excluding COVID-19. In addition to a well-balanced diet and regular exercise, healing crystals can help you prevent and fight these big six killers.

Concern	Top 3 Healing Stones		
Heart Disease Cardiovascular disease is the number one killer of Americans. It is linked to diet, lifestyle, and cholesterol levels. We would all do well to follow our intuition as we bring these crystals into our life!	**Blue Apatite** Raises metabolism and stabilizes blood pressure	**Green Aventurine** Lowers cholesterol and promotes heart health	**Rose Quartz** Powerfully heals and strengthens the heart
Cancer Malignant cells attack the body from within, draining our life force. Cancer is so commonplace, it seems this cruel disease touches everyone's lives in some way. Combine these stones with a stone that directs its energy to the location of the cancer in the body.	**Clear Quartz** The master healer	**Malachite** Powerfully regenerative; soothes chemotherapy symptoms	**Selenite** Stops free radicals, preventing cancer at its source

Concern	*Top 3 Healing Stones*		
Stroke A stroke occurs when oxygen is cut off from your brain. Brain cells begin to die within minutes. Prevent strokes and heal from past episodes with these stones.	**Amber** Strengthens brain tissue	**Watermelon Tourmaline** Encourages nerve regeneration	**Hematite** Promotes blood circulation, preventing stroke
Chronic Lower Respiratory Diseases This category of top killers includes chronic bronchitis, emphysema, and asthma. Fortunately, crystals can facilitate healing for the lungs and breath.	**Moss Agate** Powerful lung healing	**Pyrite** Clears the lungs, especially bronchitis	**Amethyst** Promotes deep, healing breaths
Alzheimer's Alzheimer's is a progressive disease that first kills the connections between brain cells before attacking the cells themselves.	**Lepidolite** Relieves Alzheimer's symptoms	**Rhodonite** Strengthens the senses	**Black Tourmaline** Grounding and protective

Concern	Top 3 Healing Stones		
Diabetes Diabetes is a group of disorders that affect the way the body processes sugar. Regardless of the type of diabetes, crystals can help relieve symptoms and change your blood sugar levels.	**Sodalite** Cleanses toxins and stabilized blood sugar 	**Citrine** Curbs sugar cravings 	**Bloodstone** Great for blood health of all kinds

Parts of the Body

Rather than choosing a crystal based on an ailment, you may choose a crystal for the part of the body to which it correlates. As always, rely on your intuition when choosing the right healing stones for you, and don't be afraid to experiment. You may find powerful effects by combining two crystals in this way. For example, in the case of brain cancer, combine malachite with hematite.

Body Part	Top 3 Healing Stones		
Brain & Nervous System In addition to these stones, any crystal that taps into the Third Eye or pineal gland is great for targeting the brain and nervous system.	**Hematite** The "stone of the mind" 	**Amethyst** Calms nervous system and promotes brain health 	**Green Aventurine** Stabilizes the nervous system

Body Part	*Top 3 Healing Stones*		
Spine Spinal concerns range from slipped discs to scoliosis to plain old back pain. These crystals will target your neck and back to deliver direct healing.	**Azurite** Treats ailments of the vertebrae	**Selenite** Aligns the spinal column	**Carnelian** Heals lower back pain
Bones & Joints Minerals rich in calcium are a natural choice for bone health, while any crystal that targets inflammation will relieve joint pains.	**Blue Apatite** Relieves joint pain	**Blue Lace Agate** Heals broken bones and encourages bone growth	**Garnet** Promotes regeneration and treats inflammation
Respiratory System The respiratory system includes your lungs, airways, and blood vessels. This bodily system is susceptible to infection and disease, but these crystals can target it directly!	**Apophyllite** Excellent for the airways and sinuses	**Moss Agate** Targets the lungs	**Amber** Great for the breath and allergic reactions

Body Part	*Top 3 Healing Stones*		
Cardiovascular System Your cardiovascular system includes your heart, blood, and blood vessels. Any stone that connects to your heart chakra will be beneficial for targeting this area.	**Rose Quartz** The quintessential heart healer	**Bloodstone** Targets the blood	**Rhodochrosite** Clears blockages and strengthens the heart
Digestive System Digestive symptoms vary, and it's quite common to experience them. Luckily, any crystal corresponding to the solar plexus chakra can help.	**Citrine** Stimulates digestion	**Chrysoprase** Detoxes system and eases digestion	**Peridot** Relieves gut and bowel pain
Reproductive System The reproductive system includes internal and external sex organs. Stones that target the sacral chakra will be particularly effective against ailments of this bodily system.	**Moonstone** Heals female organs and promotes fertility	**Carnelian** Stimulates reproductive organs	**Unakite** Clears the sacral chakra

Body Part	*Top 3 Healing Stones*		
Skin Skin problems affect many of us. Let your intuition guide you toward the crystal that will help with your particular skin concerns.	**Jade** Anti-aging properties	**Clear Quartz** Detox and clarify	**Blue Lace Agate** Targets the skin

Common Ailments

Crystal healing is by no means limited to fighting major diseases. The table below contains my recommendations for healing stones to help with a wide variety of common, minor ailments.

Concern	*Top 3 Healing Stones*		
Headache Headaches have many causes. Stress is one of them, and it's no wonder headaches are common today. Fortunately, crystals are here to relieve stress, tension, and pain.	**Amethyst** Headache healing superstar!	**Blue Dumortierite** Relieves headache and promotes relaxation	**Angelite** Best for tension headaches

Concern	*Top 3 Healing Stones*		
Sinus Congestion A common symptom of seasonal allergies as well as cold and flu, these crystals will help clear up sinus congestion.	**Green Aventurine** Powerful inflammation relief	**Apophyllite** Opens/clears the airways	**Sodalite** Relieves nasal congestion
Cough & Sore Throat Whether from allergies or illness, any stone indicated for the throat chakra would be an ideal choice for sore throat and chest congestion. These are my top three picks!	**Aquamarine** Treats throat pain & swelling	**Lapis Lazuli** Cleanses throat & soothes vocal chords	**Sodalite** Relieves throat/chest congestion
Nausea & Vomiting In general, crystals connected to the solar plexus chakra work well for common stomach ailments. Here are a few favorites.	**Fire Agate** For any type of stomach upset	**Orange Calcite** Soothes nausea and treats ulcers	**Citrine** Encourages proper digestion and stops vomiting

Concern	*Top 3 Healing Stones*		
Allergic Reactions Whether it's a swollen throat or itchy skin, crystals are here to ease your allergy symptoms.	**Apophyllite** Ideal for seasonal allergies	**Rhodonite** Soothes itchy skin	**Clear Quartz** Powerful immunotherapy
Infection For best results, combine these infection-fighting stones with crystals that target the area of infection.	**Shungite** Powerful cleansing for bacterial or viral infections	**White Opal** Clears infection from the body	**Blue Kyanite** Clears infections *and* relieves associated pain
Fatigue When you find yourself feeling sluggish and run-down, these energizing crystals are here to save the day!	**Vanadinite** Powerfully physical energizing	**Garnet** Gives your brain a boost, like a good cup of joe!	**Citrine** Bright and energizing

Concern	Top 3 Healing Stones		
Urinary Health From kidney stones to overactive bladders, these crystals can help keep your urinary system in top shape.	**Carnelian** Encourages energy flow through urinary tract	**Amber** Targets bladder and kidneys—perfect for stones	**Dalmatian Jasper** Treats urinary incontinence
Bowel Movements We all have trouble with bowel movements from time to time. Crystals can help balance your bowels in either direction.	**Red Jasper** Relieves diarrhea	**Pyrite** Prevents incontinence	**Green Calcite** Gently relieves constipation
Muscle Soreness Sore muscles are a common symptom of overexertion as well as a host of minor illnesses, like the flu. Fortunately, crystals can target these symptoms directly.	**Blue Dumortierite** Relaxes muscles to aid pain relief	**Purple Fluorite** Soothes the muscles	**Fuchsite** Relieves pain and encourages muscle recuperation

Chronic Illnesses

Outside of the "big six," many of us suffer from other chronic conditions that are rarely cured by modern medicine, only eased. These stones can help you fight chronic illnesses.

Concern	Top 3 Healing Stones		
Blood Disorders Many iron-containing crystals are ideal for treating disorders of the blood, from anemia to clots.	**Bloodstone** Treats *any* blood-related issue	**Hematite** Perfect for all types of anemia	**Black Opal** Treats and prevents blood clots, including deep vein thrombosis
Autoimmune Disorders This is a broad category of disorders in which your immune system effectively attacks the body. Fortunately, these crystals work directly on the immune system.	**Clear Quartz** For any and all immune difficulties	**Smoky Quartz** Nervous system strengthening—for multiple sclerosis or myasthenia gravis	**Aquamarine** Calms overactive immune system; good for lupus and celiac

Concern	Top 3 Healing Stones		
Bone & Joint Disorders Chronic illnesses of the bones and joints can be very painful. Here are my top three choices for healing the effects of these disorders.	**Howlite** Encourages bone density—ideal for osteoporosis	**Obsidian** Strengthens joints; great for arthritis relief	**Amazonite** Strengthens brittle bones, such as osteogenesis
Dermatological Conditions From acne to psoriasis, you can use these crystals directly on the affected areas of the skin for best results.	**Peridot** Treats acne, especially cystic	**Blue Lace Agate** Soothes the redness, pain, and itching of psoriasis	**Jade** Ideal for easing rosacea
Neurological Disorders Diseases that attack the central nervous system are not uncommon, and they vary greatly. Here are some of the best stones to help chronic nerve problems.	**Muscovite** Strengthens nervous system	**Sugilite** For Huntington's disease and muscular dystrophy	**Lepidolite** Relaxes nervous system—ideal for epilepsy and seizures

Concern	*Top 3 Healing Stones*		
Chronic Pain A number of conditions can cause chronic pain. In addition to the top pain relieving stones, try these to target your specific cause.	**Purple Fluorite** Ideal for fibromyalgia	**Azurite** Ideal for sciatica	**Kunzite** Ideal for migraines
Imbalanced Cholesterol & Blood Pressure High cholesterol and hypertension are treatable problems—but left untreated, they can lead to much worse.	**Green Aventurine** Lowers bad cholesterol and raises good cholesterol	**Mangano Calcite** Treats hypertension	**Rhodochrosite** Balances blood pressure; can be used to raise or lower it as needed
Adrenal Disorders The adrenal glands are located near the kidneys and regulate the hormones adrenaline and cortisol. Crystals related to the sacral chakra are great choices here.	**Chrysocolla** Ideal for chronic kidney disease	**Jade** Regulates adrenal gland to treat Addison's and Cushing's	**Carnelian** Fortifies and cleanses adrenal glands

Concern	*Top 3 Healing Stones*		
Weight and Nutrition Whether you struggle with obesity or nutritional deficiency, these stones can bring balance to your body.	**Iolite** For weight loss 	**Unakite** For weight gain 	**Turquoise** Helps the body absorb and retain nutrients
Thyroid Disorders Part of the endocrine system, the thyroid gland regulates hormones that control metabolism. When your thyroid is out of balance, these stones can bring it back to center.	**Aquamarine** Balances thyroid in either direction 	**Lapis Lazuli** Energizes sluggish thyroid (hypothyroidism) 	**Blue Lace Agate** Calms overactive thyroid (hyperthyroidism)

Men's & Women's Health

Women and men face specific challenges based on our differing reproductive systems. These crystals are here for you to turn to when you need help with sexual function.

Concern	Top 3 Healing Stones		
Menstrual Troubles From PMS to PCOS, crystals can help ease troublesome menstrual period problems.	**Malachite** For premenstrual symptoms, including cramps	**Wulfenite** Regulates period; ideal for polycystic ovarian syndrome	**Bloodstone** For heavy menstrual flow
Erectile & Prostate Health Many men suffer from reproductive issues. It's nothing to be ashamed about; reach for one of these stones for help!	**Chrysoprase** Promotes prostate health	**Carnelian** Encourages blood flow to the penis	**Tiger's Eye** Boosts testosterone
Infertility & Pregnancy Health Crystals can both promote fertility and keep you and your baby healthy throughout your pregnancy.	**Moonstone** The quintessential fertility enhancer	**Aquamarine** Prevents miscarriage	**Unakite** Encourages healthy pregnancy

Concern	Top 3 Healing Stones		
Low Libido & Anorgasmia Sexual health is important to our overall wellbeing. These stones can help you find a satisfying sex life.	**Shiva Lingam** Boosts libido for both men and women	**Fire Agate** Raises sexual energies	**Rhodonite** Boosts sexual pleasure and intimacy

Mental Acuity

There are so many things in life that cause our mental abilities to lag, and situations in which we need a boost. These crystals will directly target your mind to help you be your best intellectual self.

Concern	Top 3 Healing Stones		
Brain Fog If you're struggling to think straight, concentrate, or come to a conclusion, these stones are a perfect aid.	**Blue Apatite** Clears confusion	**Clear Quartz** Enhances concentration	**Azurite** Stimulates intellect

Concern	*Top 3 Healing Stones*		
Memory Loss Memory loss can have a number of causes. Regardless of the source, these crystals will help you tap into the memory centers of your brain.	**Hematite** The quintessential memory stone	**Howlite** Promotes memory	**Pyrite** Encourages recall
Studying & Test Taking Turn to these stones anytime you need your mind at its sharpest and distractions at a minimum.	**Green Fluorite** The best stone for students!	**Garnet** Energizes the mind	**Amazonite** Alleviates test anxiety
Senility & Dementia It's painful to watch a loved one's mental faculties degrade with age and disease. Fortunately, these crystals can stave off mental degeneration.	**Pink Tourmaline** Aids understanding and relieves paranoia	**Rhodonite** Helps one stay in touch with themselves	**Blue Kyanite** Encourages self-expression

Unbalanced Moods & Unquiet Thoughts

Many of us struggle with mental health issues and sensory problems that inhibit our thought processes. It's nothing to be ashamed of; reach for these stones for some help getting back to your best self.

Concern	*Top 3 Healing Stones*		
Chronic Stress Crystal healing is one of the very best treatments for chronic stress, as so many stones impart calm and relieve tension. Here are a few favorites.	**Lapis Lazuli** Powerful de-stresser, calms the mind	**Mookaite** Nurturing and calming	**Purple Fluorite** Relieves mental and physical symptoms of stress
Substance Abuse Substance abuse can range from alcoholism to illicit drug use. These crystals can help overcome the desire to use drugs and alcohol.	**Amethyst** The sobriety stone—top choice for addictions.	**Iolite** Heals an addictive personality	**Hematite** Stops compulsive drug use
Depression Depression is a mood disorder characterized by anhedonia, fatigue, and listlessness. Depression can be situational or chronic; many sufferers are high functioning.	**Carnelian** Warm & comforting	**Citrine** Bright & energizing	**Smoky Quartz** Grounding; dispels intrusive thoughts

Concern	*Top 3 Healing Stones*		
Bipolar Disorder In bipolar disorder (also called manic depressive disorder), episodes of depression are interspersed with periods of excessive energy and delusions of grandeur, called mania.	**Blue Dumortierite** Takes the edge off of extreme emotions	**Purple Fluorite** Provides mental clarity	**Tiger's Eye** Balances mood swings
Anxiety & Panic Attacks Anxiety is characterized by excessive dread, which activates a "fight or flight" nervous response. People with anxiety disorders may appear high-functioning but are suffering constantly beneath the surface.	**Amethyst** Induces tranquility; quiets racing thoughts	**Chrysocolla** Dispels fear and vanquishes phobias	**Howlite** Grounds the mind *and* body
Sensory Challenges Common among neurodivergent people, such as with autism and ADHD, a heightened sensitivity to the world around you can make concentration and emotional stability seem impossible to reach.	**Clear Quartz** Powerfully cleansing and stabilizing	**Blue Dumortierite** Calms you and helps you verbalize what's wrong	**Sugilite** Clears distracting energies, promoting focus

Sleep & Dreams

Sleep is essential to our health. Without regular, restful sleep, all the systems of the body suffer—as do our emotions. Healing stones can help you get the quality rest you need.

Concern	Top 3 Healing Stones		
Sleeplessness & Poor Quality Sleep Insomnia can be a symptom of a larger illness, but it's also its own beast. No matter the source, these crystals will help you catch some Zs.	**Amethyst** Treats insomnia	**Chrysoprase** Promotes restful sleep	**Moonstone** Gently lulls you to sleep
Nightmares Nightmares can disrupt our sleep and cause mental distress even during waking hours. These crystals will encourage peaceful rather than bad dreams.	**Smoky Quartz** Prevents nightmares	**Hematite** Protects against nightmares and sleep terrors	**Mangano Calcite** Encourages beautiful dreams
Lucid & Astral Dreams Sleep can also be a time of great spiritual significance. Lucid and astral dreaming practices are within your reach with the aid of these stones.	**Celestite** Encourages lucidity during dreams	**Lepidolite** Enhances astral travel	**Labradorite** Guides one through dreams

Relationships

Our personal relationships are paramount to our emotional health, but even the best relationships experience rocky times. Let your intuition guide you toward the stones that will help you cultivate, nurture, and heal your relationships.

Concern	Top 3 Healing Stones		
Self Love & Self Care The most important relationship you'll have in your life is your relationship with yourself.	**Rose Quartz** Encourages self-love and self-acceptance	**Rhodochrosite** Cultivates compassion for the self	**Mangano Calcite** Boost self-esteem
Dating Whether you're searching for Mr. or Mrs. Right, turn to these crystals for help navigating the dating world.	**Jade** Welcomes new love into your life	**Garnet** Ignites attraction	**Green Aventurine** For good luck finding the one
Marriage Long-term partnership can bring incredible blessings to your life, as well as potential for personal growth—but a happy marriage takes hard work. These crystals will help you maintain yours.	**Amazonite** Maintains emotional bonds	**Turquoise** Helps you stay calm during conflict	**Watermelon Tourmaline** Harmonizes and balances your energies as a couple

Concern	Top 3 Healing Stones		
Friendships Who would we be without our friends? They lift us up when we're down and share in our joys. Friends stay while lovers may come and go. Use these stones to nurture your platonic relationships.	**Watermelon Tourmaline** Attracts new friendships	**Sodalite** Aids in healthy, honest communication	**Golden Topaz** For relationships built on joy
Anger & Forgiveness When there is a disagreement or hurt feelings, relationships can suffer and even fail. These crystals can help you heal your connections to others when they are under duress.	**Blue Lace Agate** Neutralizes anger while allowing you to speak from your heart	**Muscovite** Calms anger and eases tensions	**Angelite** Helps you forgive yourself and others

Major Life Changes & Challenges

Change is inevitable, but it can be difficult to embrace and work through. I've listed crystals here to help guide you through some of the biggest shake-ups we experience in our lives.

Concern	*Top 3 Healing Stones*		
Grief & Loss Losing someone you love is traumatic. Grief stays with us a long time as we heal and grow around our loss. Crystals can help us process our feelings and ease the pain of mourning.	**Amethyst** Gently guides you through the grieving process	**Lepidolite** This transition stone helps you to let go of suffering	**Black Tourmaline** Keeps you grounded in the now rather than losing yourself to mourning
Moving Homes Moving homes is well documented as one of the top sources of stress in a person's lifetime. These crystals can help you stay afloat during this period of intense change.	**Lepidolite** Eases you through the transition	**Malachite** Enables you to adapt to the change	**Bloodstone** Grounds you in your new home
A New Job Starting a new job is an exciting time, but it can also be highly stressful. Use these stones to make the best of it.	**Moonstone** Blessings for new beginnings	**Carnelian** Promotes career success	**Peridot** Boosts self-confidence

Concern	Top 3 Healing Stones		
Breakups & Divorce It can be incredibly painful to end a relationship. Allow yourself time to grieve, and keep these crystals close to help you through. It's always darkest before dawn.	**Chrysoprase** Helps you find your own inner strength	**Moss Agate** Balances the painful emotions of a break-up	**Selenite** Clear out old relationship energies

Practical Crystal Shapes

Crystals come in a wide variety of natural forms, as detailed above—but another factor to consider when discussing crystal shapes is human intervention. Many crystals (especially those that are cryptocrystalline in nature) are commonly purchased as cut and polished stones, and each particular shape has specific metaphysical properties. Even when a specimen is natural, its macro shape imparts meaning. Understanding what these shapes mean can add another level of precision to your crystal healing practice.

Shape	Example	Properties & Uses
Tower Many prismatic crystals naturally terminate in points. When the bottom of the crystal is flattened so that it can stand straight on a surface, this is called a tower.		• Energy is directed upwards and outwards • Natural prismatic termination amplifies the crystal's energy • Perfect for center of a crystal altar • Great for meditation, either held in the hand or sat on the ground before you

Shape	Example	Properties & Uses
Cluster or Geode A naturally forming cluster of many small crystals; when the crystals are especially tiny, this is called "druzy."		• The many clustered prisms super-charge the energy of the stone • Perfect for transmuting energies into a space rather than a person—top choice for cleansing a room or home • Can place smaller crystals within/atop the cluster
Sphere A stone that has been cut and polished into a perfect sphere or globe, like a "crystal ball."		• Emits energy from all sides • Harmonious and balanced energy • Can be used for scrying (a form of divination that involves staring into a surface until visions appear) • Perfect for massage therapy • Ideal for holding during meditation
Egg Similar to a sphere, but oblong—literally shaped like an egg!		• Emits energy from all sides • Represents birth/rebirth—perfect for fertility stones • Perfect for reflexology, as both the broad and smaller ends can be used for message
Pyramid While some crystals have a natural pyramidal habit, most pyramids found in crystal shops have been cut and polished to this recognizable shape.		• Duality of solid, grounded base and upward point makes this shape ideal for meditative practice • Perfect for chakra work • Ideal at the center of a crystal grid

Shape	Example	Properties & Uses
Wand Similar to a crystal tower without the flattened bottom. Sometimes the points are smoothed and rounded, making them ideal for massage.		• Enables you to direct energy where it is needed • Good for "drawing" symbols or sigils in the air to manifest your intentions • Good for charging and cleansing other crystals • Rounded ends are great for message
Palm Stone Something of a blanket term, a palm stone is any smoothed, relatively-flat shape that can fit in the hand.		• Easy to carry with you throughout the day • Great for putting under your pillow to sleep • Ideal for holding during meditation—or at any time of day when you need a boost
Free-Form Often crystals are cut into irregular, smoothed shapes, with or without one or more flat sides. This is typically done based on the shape of the original specimen.		• No specific metaphysical properties due to their varying shapes • Make great statement pieces in the home • Perfect for meditating with • Doubles as paperweight or bookend if large enough

Part III

Advanced Instruction: Crystal Healing Therapies

Chapter Five

From Root to Crown: Crystals and the Seven Chakras

If you've taken a yoga class, you've probably opened your heart chakra or meditated on your third eye. These are two of the seven major chakras, the energy centers of our bodies. They are points along the center axis of the human body where specific energies are densely concentrated, the ancient wisdom of which was recorded around 1500 B.C.E. in India as part of the Vedic texts.

These energy centers correspond with specific organs, emotions, and spiritual states of being, and within each chakra is *prana*: our very lifeforce and the ultimate in healing energy. Within our very bodies is the healing power we need to stay happy and healthy physically, mentally, and emotionally—as long as our chakras remain open and aligned.

The problem is that emotional upheavals, physical illnesses, and spiritual stagnation can cause the chakras or energy centers to become blocked, preventing their healing energy from spreading to the corresponding bodily systems. Chakra blockages can manifest as a myriad of negative effects, and other chakras can become overactive in response, leading to all sorts of bodily and spiritual havoc.

The seven chakras, from bottom to top, are the root, sacral, solar plexus, heart, throat, third eye, and crown. Figure 5 below shows the locations of the chakras in the body, as well as their corresponding colors and the major physical, spiritual, and emotional qualities they rule.

Crystals have a powerful association with the seven chakras. Because crystals heal through energy transfer and the chakras are energy epicenters, healing stones can be utilized to unblock, stabilize, and realign the chakras. In this chapter, I'll teach you how to recognize chakra blockages and how to use your crystal collection to clear your full-body energy flow.

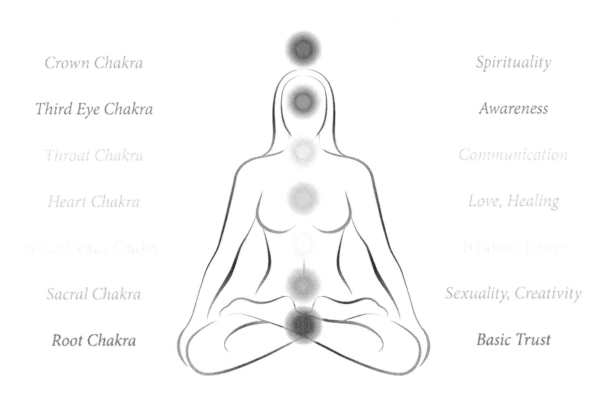

Crown Chakra

Third Eye Chakra

Throat Chakra

Heart Chakra

Solar Plexus Chakra

Sacral Chakra

Root Chakra

Spirituality

Awareness

Communication

Love, Healing

Wisdom, Power

Sexuality, Creativity

Basic Trust

Figure 5: The seven chakras or energy epicenters of the body.

Diagnosing Blocked Chakras

Each chakra rules both a part of the body and a specific area of your psyche. When a chakra becomes blocked, the energy in that area of the self is not flowing as it should be. Imagine that the energy flow in your body is a rushing stream; blockages to your chakra are like rocks that dam the flow of water. This energy blockage can manifest in a variety of physical, mental, and spiritual symptoms.

You can diagnose a blocked chakra by matching any symptoms you may be experiencing with the chakra that rules that area of the body, mind, and spirit. The table below lists some common symptoms of a blockage of each chakra, as well as signs that indicate your chakras are open and letting your vital life energy flow freely as intended.

Chakra	Signs It's Blocked	Signs It's Open
Root Basic trust, reproductive glands	• You have not healed from a traumatic childhood experience • You feel self-hatred and do not take care of your body • You're in "survival mode" all of the time, never truly thriving • You experience recurrent financial difficulty • You feel sluggish, fatigued, and unmotivated	• You cultivate healthy relationships with your family and close friends • You feel safe, cared for, wanted, and loved • You love your body and feel thankful for all that it does for you • You act confidently with money
Sacral Creativity, adrenal glands	• You have trouble with sexual intimacy, or you confuse sex with love • You have not healed from past abuse • You find yourself in toxic relationship after toxic relationship • You are experiencing a creative block	• You have a healthy, fulfilled sex life • Your creative ideas flow freely and easily • You find pleasure and joy in life every day
Solar Plexus Power, pancreas	• You feel powerless, like a victim of circumstance • You have low self-esteem • You feel stuck in your life • You've lost sight of your dreams and goals • You experience anxiety, stomach cramps, or nausea	• You feel called to use your power for good, to make the world a better place • You have a healthy sense of self-esteem and confidence in your abilities • You don't seek the validation or approval of others

Chakra	*Signs It's Blocked*	*Signs It's Open*
Heart Love, thymus gland	• You have closed yourself off from others or fear commitment • You are overly focused on people pleasing • You're holding grudges or feel unable to move on from past mistakes • You are suffering from chest pain or have difficulty breathing	• You feel good in your relationships with others • You can receive compliments and accept love from others easily • You feel gratitude and love your life • You deeply appreciate the contributions of others
Throat Communication, thyroid gland	• You feel afraid of speaking your truth • You act as a "doormat" and go along with others to avoid breaking the peace • You get frustrated because people don't seem to be hearing what you have to say • You suffer thyroid disorder, a sore throat, or tension in the neck and jaw	• You speak directly from the heart with confidence • You don't talk negatively about others or gossip • You take responsibility for communicating and understand that other people are not mind readers
Third Eye Awareness, pineal gland	• Your inner voice is quiet, and you can't connect to your intuition • You experience headaches, insomnia, or nightmares • You have difficulty concentrating • You experience persistent negative thoughts or paranoia	• You feel peace and wholeness knowing you have a greater purpose • You are in touch with your intuition • You trust your instincts and intellect, and your mind is quiet of negative thoughts
Crown Spirituality, pituitary	• You're disconnected from your spiritual side • You feel unworthy of good things • You behave materialistically and cling tightly to money and material possessions • You experience migraines	• You feel connected to a higher power • You know your worth as a human being • You embrace your inner child • You feel gratitude and universal love

What Causes a Blocked Chakra?

Blockages can have physical, emotional, or spiritual causes. An injury or illness can cause a blocked chakra, as can general poor health, such as with a sedentary lifestyle or junk food diet. An upheaval in your life can send your chakras out of balance quicker than anything! Many blockages, especially of the lower chakras, are caused by stress and anxiety. These emotions have a strong effect on our physical bodies, causing muscles to tense and restricting the flow of prana through the body. Long-term exposure to these emotions, such as with abuse and trauma, compounds the problem.

In most cases, you are not to blame for a blocked chakra, so you shouldn't be hard on yourself—but you do have the power within you to get your prana flowing again!

Unblocking & Aligning the Chakras with Crystals

Crystal healing is perhaps the best way to heal a blocked chakra, and the process is quite simple—you place a healing stone on the body over the chakra that needs healing. The trick of it is to choose a stone whose energies correspond to the chakra you need to unblock.

Crystals and stones correspond with the chakras based primarily on the color of the stone. Think of it this way: the energies in the stone that give the crystal its color are the same energies contained within the corresponding chakra. In addition to the rainbow of colors, white or clear stones typically resonate with the crown chakra, while black and brown stones are most often connected to the root chakra. Pink stones are typically given to the heart chakra.

The table below gives you some of the crystals most strongly associated with each chakra. You can always refer back to Chapter 3 to find the corresponding chakra for every crystal listed. For best results, choose a crystal that corresponds both to the chakra in question *and* to the specific symptoms you are experiencing.

Above all, though, listen to your gut (or in this case, your solar plexus)! If your instincts draw you to a certain crystal, there's a good reason for it.

Chakra	Top 3 Healing Stones		
Root Basic needs/trust; reds, black, some browns, and some pinks 	**Tiger's Eye** Highly grounding and protective 	**Hematite** Purifies the blood; promotes endurance 	**Fire Agate** Energizes the body; curbs sugar cravings
Sacral Creativity and sexuality; yellow-gold to deep orange, most browns 	**Orange Calcite** Enhances creativity; heals the reproductive system 	**Carnelian** Boosts libido; treats kidneys, bladder, and lower back pain 	**Sunstone** Invigorating; induces feelings of satisfaction
Solar Plexus Power/gut and urinary tract; light yellow to golden yellow 	**Amber** Highly empowering; heals kidneys, bladder, and gallbladder 	**Golden Topaz** Heals the liver; imparts drive and motivation 	**Citrine** Stabilizes blood sugar; stimulates digestion; raises self-esteem

Chakra	Top 3 Healing Stones		
Heart Love/heart and lungs; all shades of green, most pinks 	**Rose Quartz** The stone of unconditional love; relieves chest pain 	**Green Aventurine** Lowers cholesterol and blood pressure; promotes compassion 	**Peridot** Releases anger, resentment, and jealousy
Throat Communication/thyroid and lymph nodes; deep blue to aqua blue 	**Aquamarine** Balances thyroid; soothes sore and swollen throat 	**Sodalite** Encourages clear communication 	**Turquoise** Helps you articulate your thoughts
Third Eye Awareness/pineal gland; blue-violet to indigo 	**Azurite** Opens mind to new ideas and perspectives; targets brain stem and cerebellum 	**Purple Fluorite** Treats mental and mood disorders of all kinds; improves mental acuity; relieves headaches 	**Celestite** Awakens intuition; promotes mindfulness; relaxes nerves

Chakra	*Top 3 Healing Stones*		
Crown Spirituality/pituitary gland; purple/violet, white, or clear	**Amethyst** Relieves migraines; induces tranquility; connects you to the spirit realm	**Clear Quartz** Balances all chakras; brings mind, body, and spirit into alignment	**Selenite** Spiritually cleansing; aligns the spinal column and heals the nervous system

When I first began to heal my body, head, and heart with crystals, I discovered that I had a *serious* blockage of my crown chakra. I had lost touch with my spiritual side; I felt cynical, lost, and alone in the universe.

I began meditating for a few minutes every day in a seated position with a selenite wand resting on top of my head and drank water charged with amethyst crystals. Over time, I felt my sense of faith grow stronger, and a deep peace began to settle into my soul—even in the face of the cancer I was fighting.

While this spiritual healing was amazing in itself, I also began to notice that I felt better all over, both physically and emotionally. Mysterious aches and pains throughout my body vanished; I had more energy and woke up every day excited to be alive. Opening my crown chakra allowed life force to flow through my entire system that I didn't even realize had been off balance!

Full-Body Crystal Grid

If one chakra is blocked—especially one of the lower chakras—this can throw off the balance of the others. For this reason, when you're working on one chakra, it is good practice to pay mind to the others.

One way to heal all chakras at once is with a full-body crystal grid. This is similar to the crystal grid mentioned in Chapter 2, but rather than a geometric grid on a piece of cloth, here, *you* are the cloth, and your chakras are the points of the grid. Figure 6 below illustrates the idea.

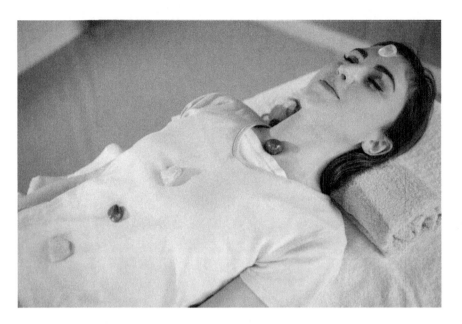

Figure 6: A woman with a full-body crystal grid, including green calcite at her heart chakra and malachite at her solar plexus chakra.

You may find it's easier to do this practice with the help of a friend. Before beginning, choose at least one crystal from your collection for each of the seven chakras.

First, set the mood, and set your intention. Find a comfortable place to lay flat on your back where you can remain still for 30 minutes. Turn the lights down, light some candles or incense, maybe play some relaxing music, and focus on your intention. Your intention or affirmation can be something simple and straightforward (e.g., "Prana flows through me") or more specific (e.g., "I welcome love into my life and give it back to the universe").

Next, with the help of a friend if needed, place your chosen crystals atop each of the energy points indicated below in Figure 7 (or as close as you can get).

Relax here and breathe deeply and evenly. Count to four on the inhale, pause, and count to five on the exhale. Do this for a few repetitions until you begin to enter a meditative state.

Then, spend a few minutes meditating on each one of your chakras, beginning with the root. Visualize the colorful energy of each crystal as it seeps into your body. Picture the energy as it flows freely from the crystal to your chakra and focus on that part of your body— *see* the healing happening in your mind's eye. All the while, keep breathing, and repeat to yourself the intention you set earlier.

Once you reach the crown chakra and have fully visualized your crystal(s) opening your crown, bring your attention back to your surroundings. You can repeat this practice as often as needed to keep your chakras open and aligned.

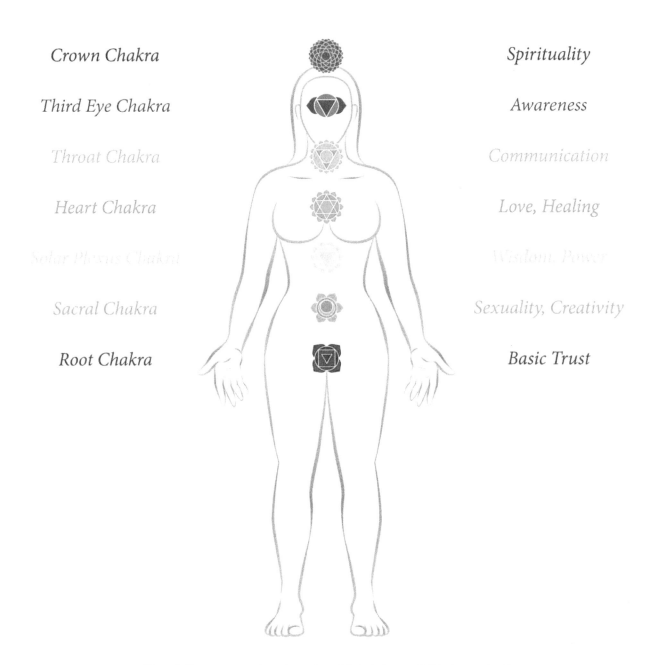

Crown Chakra — Spirituality

Third Eye Chakra — Awareness

Throat Chakra — Communication

Heart Chakra — Love, Healing

Solar Plexus Chakra — Wisdom, Power

Sacral Chakra — Sexuality, Creativity

Root Chakra — Basic Trust

Figure 7: Place your crystals on these points of the body for your full-body crystal grid.

Raising Kundalini Energy with Crystals

Kundalini is a Vedic concept closely related to the chakras. Kundalini energy is a specific type of prana that lays dormant in all of us; it is a divinely feminine and creative energy, the basis of our consciousness. The word *kundalini* in Sanskrit means "coiled snake," and it is said that this energetic serpent rests, coiled three and a half times at the base of the spine, until it is awoken and rises through the chakras, as illustrated in Figure 8 below. When this happens, it is called a kundalini awakening—an enlightenment of the mind, body, and soul.

Figure 8: Kundalini is represented by an energetic snake that lays coiled at the root chakra.
In a kundalini awakening, the snake uncoils and rises through the chakras.

A kundalini awakening can happen in many different ways—through the practice of kundalini yoga, through meditation, and spontaneously for some! When it does, most people report accompanying physical sensations—a heat in the body, tingling feelings, a tensing of muscles, laughter and joy, to name a few—and spiritual visions.

In order for kundalini to rise, all of your chakras must be open, clear, and aligned—so it's best not to work with kundalini energy unless and until you feel confident that there are no lingering energetic blocks. Some have reported long-term negative side effects from a kundalini awakening that they were not prepared for.

Kundalini Awakening Meditation

There is one healing crystal in particular that is perfect for encouraging a kundalini awakening: shiva lingam. This intensely holy stone is shaped like an elongated egg and represents divine creation. If you feel you're ready to seek your kundalini awakening, try this meditation practice.

As before, set the mood, and set your intention. Find a comfortable place to sit cross-legged, back straight, or lay flat on your back. Turn the lights down (or cover your eyes with an eye pillow), light some candles or incense, play some relaxing music, and focus on your intention. (Something like, "The kundalini rises in me, from root to crown" will do.)

Place a shiva lingam stone at or near your root chakra; if you have a second specimen, you can place it on your crown, or use selenite or clear quartz, instead.

As with the chakra-opening practice, breathe deeply and evenly. Count to four on the inhale, pause, and count to five on the exhale. Do this for a few repetitions until you begin to enter a meditative state.

Then, visualize the coiled snake at the base of your spine. Feel the energy of the shiva lingam at your root chakra as it stirs the serpent to wake. Picture clearly in your mind the serpent slowly beginning to uncoil and slither up your spine, drawn to the crystal at your crown. As the snake passes each chakra in your mind's eye, pause and meditate on that chakra. Simply let any emotions or physical sensations that come up *be*; acknowledge them, but do not focus on them. Remain focused on your breathing and your visualizations.

I experienced a kundalini awakening myself using this method. During the meditation, I had the strange sense that I couldn't feel my feet or legs at all—they went numb—but a fiery energy rose through the rest of my body. When I brought myself back to the physical world, all the colors before me seemed brighter, and I could not stop smiling! I have to credit much of my continued inner peace and powers of manifestation to this experience.

While there is much more to know about the chakras, this introduction is enough to begin your journey to holistic wellness through the magic of prana, kundalini, and crystals. Now, let's take a look at how crystals can benefit another popular energy healing practice: reiki.

Chapter Six

Healing Hands: An Introduction to Reiki Stones

Reiki is a form of hands-on energy healing that originated in Japan. There, on Mt. Kurama in the early twentieth century, Mikao Usui fasted and prayed for 21 days, and when he came down from the mountain, he brought the divine healing practice of reiki with him.

The word "reiki" comprises two Japanese *kanji* or characters: *rei* (霊), which refers to a higher power or divine spirit, and *ki* (気), or life force (equivalent to *chi* in Chinese or *prana* in Vedic teachings)—so "reiki" means something akin to "divinely guided life energy." The moniker is fitting; what distinguishes reiki from other types of healing-with-hands is that the power comes not from the healer but from the universe.

Reiki practitioners channelize life force energy, typically through their hands as shown in Figure 9, to promote relaxation. Reiki itself doesn't cure disease or wounds so much as it relaxes the body and spirit, releasing tension and promoting balance, which in turn encourages your body's own healing capacities to work at their maximum. Some of the major benefits of reiki healing include:

- Improved mood
- Emotional well-being
- Stress reduction
- Relief from insomnia
- Lowered blood pressure
- Pain relief
- Mitigation of anxiety

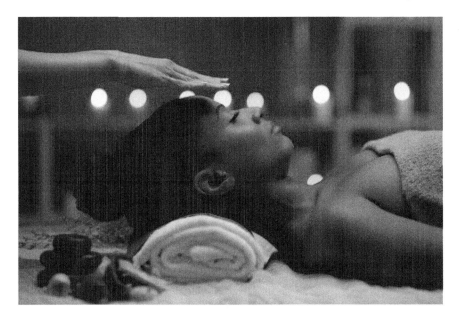

Figure 9: A reiki practitioner holds her hands just above a patient's forehead, as the patient relaxes on a massage table.

There are five philosophical principles of reiki meant to provide guidance for the practitioner. These principles are like affirmations, and in order to properly channel reiki (and to maintain spiritual health in general), a practitioner must strive to live their lives according to these tenets. Of course, we are all human and cannot be our best selves 100% of the time; this is why the five principles begin with "Just for today":

1. Just for today, I release angry thoughts.
2. Just for today, I release thoughts of worry.
3. Just for today, I am grateful.
4. Just for today, I do my work honestly.
5. Just for today, I am gentle to all living beings.

Over the years, as reiki has spread across the globe, many practitioners have found that their healing powers are amplified with the use of healing crystals. When a crystal or stone is used for this purpose, it is called a reiki stone.

The healing powers of reiki and reiki stones are accessible to anyone. In this chapter, you'll learn how you can get started with your own reiki practice—and elevate your crystal healing in the process.

Reiju: Attunement with the Divine

Because reiki works with universal healing energies, your ability to perform reiki healing does not hinge on any innate power within you. Truly *anyone* can learn to practice reiki by channeling divine healing energies—but to open yourself up to channel the full power of reiki requires a process called attunement.

Reiju is the name for this attunement ritual in reiki. In reiju, the student remains seated in a meditative state while the teacher performs a series of specific physical movements around them. In the form of reiki popularly practiced in the western world today, the ritual of attunement may also include breathwork and the use of reiki symbols, each of which is meant to encourage a particular energetic shift. Originally, Usui did not perform movements or use symbols in reiju—he sat opposite his students and was able to attune them through meditation alone.

The goal of attunement is to open the student up to receive and channel ki from the universe. Once a student has been attuned, the power to channel reiki remains with that individual for the rest of their lives. Often, however, a student will receive multiple attunements over a long period of study in order to elevate their practice.

Is Attunement Really Necessary?

Many reiki practitioners are adamant that at least one attunement by a reiki teacher is necessary for an individual to be able to practice at all—that, without it, you won't be able to channel ki from the universe through your hands. I and many others have found this to be only partially true.

Your mileage may vary; some of us are more receptive to reiki than others, likely based on our spiritual states and how open our crown chakras are. For me, before attunement, I could tangibly *feel* the reiki coming from my hands when I positioned them right above my body and visualized the divine light channeling through me—but when I received my first attunement from a reiki master in Japan, that tangible sensation of reiki grew significantly stronger!

So, while I do recommend that you seek attunement from a reiki master (either in person or virtually), you can also try practicing reiki on yourself (and your crystals) beforehand. The difference after attunement may shock you!

A Note on Reiki Certifications

When Usui began teaching reiki to his students, he devised a system of three reiki levels—introductory, intermediate, and master—in order to help guide his followers gently through expanding their practice one step at a time—much different from our western goal of immediate gratification!

Nowadays, reiki masters offer certifications corresponding to Usui's original reiki levels. It is important to note that certification from a reiki school is not a requirement for a practitioner—only attunement or reiju is.

However, the classes offered by certification programs are invaluable to learning about reiki and growing your own practice.

If you choose to seek certification, before selecting a school or master to learn from, take your time and learn all you can about the specific reiki methods that a system uses. Reiki has branched off considerably since Usui's time, and practices vary among teachers.

Enhancing Reiki with Crystals

If the healing power of crystals comes from their own innate vibrational energies, and the healing power of reiki comes from external divine energy, it stands to reason that combining the two will multiply healing effects, as the practitioner draws energy from multiple sources. Many reiki practitioners find that they can use crystals as an "extra set of hands" when performing a reiki healing as well as encourage deeper relaxation and regeneration.

Programming Reiki Stones

The process of using healing stones in reiki is quite simple. Commonly referred to as programming a crystal, this is achieved simply by holding the stone in your hands and activating reiki as shown in Figure 10 below. The practitioner will meditate on the crystal and imbue it with channeled reiki, similarly to how the practice works when laying hands on a person. Do this until you feel the energy in your hands cooling down.

You'll want to choose a crystal whose properties align with your own healing goals—see Chapters 3 and 4— but what's most important when programming a reiki stone is to focus on your intention. You must tell the crystal (and yourself) what its purpose is for this healing session. You should be as direct as possible, and focus deeply on this intention while you channel reiki into the stone in your hands.

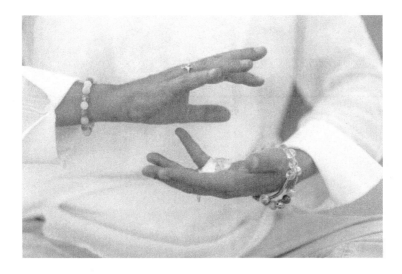

Figure 10: A reiki practitioner holds a crystal in her hands to charge it, thus creating a reiki stone.
She's also wearing several natural stone beaded bracelets.

Once the stone is programmed, you can place it on the body of the person being healed (whether that's yourself or someone else). Place the crystal as close to the source of the illness, pain, or tension as possible. This way, the stone amplifies and focuses the reiki. You can hold your healing hands above the stone or direct your hands elsewhere on the body—hence, the reiki stone allows you to channel reiki to multiple locations on the body at once.

Reiki Symbols & Reiki Stones

Reiki symbols are powerful, sacred characters that practitioners use to amplify and target reiki healing. These symbols can be used in a number of ways; traditionally, they are drawn in the air by the practitioner. They are more useful when applied to the spiritual body than the physical body. Thus, there is no need to draw symbols on a person.

Note that these symbols are incredibly sacred in reiki. Usui originally intended to keep these symbols secret from all except those ascending to reiki level 2—but as these sacred symbols are now available all over the internet, the cat is officially out of the bag! Still, reiki symbols are not to be taken lightly, nor to be used outside their intentions. You must respect these symbols and keep them sacred if you want to reap their benefits.

Combining reiki symbols with reiki stones is an excellent way to further amplify and focus reiki's healing powers. You can do this in a number of ways. Crystals are available to be purchased with these symbols etched or painted on them (such as in Figure 11), but to keep it simple, you can use a programmed reiki stone to "draw" the symbol in the air rather than using only your hands. Either way, it's essential to activate the symbol by intoning its syllables silently three times.

Figure 11: These small slices of agate have been engraved and painted with reiki symbols.

The table below shows five essential reiki symbols along with crystals whose energy complements their intent.

Symbol	Meaning	Recommended Stones		
	Cho Ku Rei The power symbol; ideal for pain relief, protection, and clearing negative energy	**Selenite**	**Tiger's Eye**	**Black Tourmaline**
	Sei He Ki The harmony symbol; ideal for purification and treating physical or emotional imbalances	**Red Jasper**	**Moss Agate**	**Blue Apatite**
	Hon Sha Ze Sho Nen The distance symbol; heals across time and space, such as with old wounds and disease prevention	**Amethyst**	**Citrine**	**Rose Quartz**
	Dai Ko Myo The master symbol; very high vibrational energy—boosts immune system and promotes self-awareness	**Clear Quartz**	**Moldavite**	**Chrysocolla**

Symbol	Meaning	Recommended Stones		
	Raku The completion symbol; highly grounding and used to end a reiki session—it encourages the body to better receive the reiki	**Hematite**	**Smoky Quartz**	**Bloodstone**

Reiki Meditation to Release Anger

One practice I found tremendously beneficial using a combination of reiki symbols and stones is a meditation on letting go of anger. When I received my cancer diagnosis, after the initial shock, anger positively clouded my mind. I was furious: with my doctors, with myself, and with the universe. So when I found reiki, the first principle ("Just for today, I release angry thoughts") spoke directly to me.

I knew I needed to let go of the misplaced rage I felt before I could move forward. If you find yourself in a situation like mine, "Just for today, I release angry thoughts" may seem like a hollow platitude—not long after you say it to yourself, an angry thought is likely to pop right back up uninvited! Try this simple meditation and see for yourself the power of reiki symbols and stones.

As with all meditations, dedicate time (30 minutes, ideally) and prepare your space. Put on some relaxing music, ensure you won't be interrupted, and lower the lights. Sit or lie down in a comfortable position. Settle in and take slow, deep breaths here. Count to four on the inhale, pause, and count to five on the exhale. Do this for ten repetitions—or more if needed to find your calm.

Next, scan your body from head to toe. Concentrate on each area of your body, one by one, and notice where you sense that you are holding tension. When you land on a spot that feels tense, stop your scan and "draw" the Sei He Ki symbol over that place on your body using your crystal of choice. (Moss agate, blue lace agate, and angelite are all great options for this.)

Visualize reiki coming down from the universe through your crown chakra to where you've drawn the symbol. Try intentionally tensing and releasing the muscles in that area to encourage relaxation. Then, continue your full-body scan and repeat this practice for any additional tense areas.

Once you've gone over your whole body, do five more repetitions of deep, counted breaths as before. Reflect on how you feel; is there lingering anger? If so, you can repeat the body scan process again. This time, use the Cho Ku Rei symbol (to increase power), and repeat either aloud or to yourself, "Just for today, I release angry thoughts."

You can repeat this practice as often as once a day if needed, but I suspect you'll find, as I did, that one iteration makes a tremendous impact!

Distance Healing with Reiki Crystals

One of the major benefits of reiki is that one needn't physically lay hands on a patient to provide healing benefits. Distance reiki is popular among experienced practitioners, but sending channeled reiki from your body across a long distance requires specific methods that we won't get into here—I recommend certification for this.

However, reiki crystals are a simple and effective way to share your healing over distances without getting into the weeds of long-distance energy transfer. Simply program your reiki crystals as you learned above; be sure to focus on your intention and specifically call to mind the person you want to heal. Then, when you're finished, give that person the stone; you can send it through the mail if you can't meet with that person face-to-face. Alternatively, you can place the programmed crystal on top of a photo of the person in question.

We have only scratched the surface of reiki in this chapter. There is much more to discover if this healing method speaks to you. Still, you should walk away from this introduction empowered. Try using reiki crystals for yourself.

Remember that the power does not come from within you; you are only the channel for the reiki. Surrendering to the power of reiki and trusting it to "do its thing," similarly to how we trust our guts when choosing crystals intuitively, will bring you amazing results!

Chapter Seven
Holistic Massage: Crystals for Reflexology

Reflexology is a truly ancient healing practice still popular worldwide today, which concentrates on massaging the feet, hands, and ears. The basic tenant of reflexology is that pressure points (or reflex areas) in the extremities correspond to zones throughout the body, connected by the nervous system. By manipulating these pressure points as shown in Figure 12, reflexologists send *chi* or life force energy (equivalent to ki and prana and also spelled "qi") through the body to the appropriate zones to facilitate targeted healing.

Figure 12: Reflexology is like a highly-targeted massage for the extremities.

The history of reflexology is a fascinating one. You probably associate reflexology with Chinese medicine, but evidence points to the first reflexology-like practice being performed by the ancient Egyptians as far back as at least 2300 B.C.E.[8] Only later, around 1000 B.C.E., is reflexology documented in Chinese texts.[9] By 1400 A.D., reflexology had spread as a practice across Europe, referred to then as "zone therapy." The father of modern reflexology was Dr. William H. Fitzgerald who, in 1917, wrote about the zones of the body and how they correspond to pressure points.

Reflexology's survival through millennia speaks to the practice's healing power. Like reiki, reflexology works primarily through the mechanisms of relaxation and stress relief, encouraging the production of pain-relieving endorphins in the body and facilitating our own natural healing processes. Some of the benefits of reflexology include:

- Relief of pain and discomfort
- Increased energy
- Detoxification of the body
- Increased blood circulation
- Enhanced mental acuity
- Boosting the metabolism

Many (myself included!) have reported additional, more targeted benefits, such as:

- Palliative care for cancer patients
- Healing viral and bacterial infections
- Treating infertility
- Relief from sleep disorders
- And many more!

Reflexology is a very safe practice with virtually no risk of adverse effects, even for the beginner, and it can be practiced by anyone, anywhere. I highly recommend you experience a reflexology session with a trained and experienced practitioner, but the concepts are simple enough that you can apply them yourself—to a lesser effect.

In this chapter, you'll learn how you can harness this ancient healing method for yourself—and how you can use your growing crystal collection to take nervous system healing to the next level!

Reflexology 101

The practice of reflexology is, at its heart, quite simple: all you do is apply message pressure with your fingers and thumbs to the appropriate area of the feet and hands. I recommend you start with the feet rather than the hands because there are so many nerve endings in the feet—plus, it's a bit challenging to massage your own dominant hand with your non-dominant one! (Although, if you find it difficult to comfortably reach your own feet due to physical challenges, the hands are a fine place to start, too.)

I recommend using lotions or oils for less friction and increased relaxation, but you can perform reflexology "dry," too. Start by "walking" your thumb up from the base of the heel to the toes—who doesn't need a good foot massage? Then, concentrate on the particular pressure points you want to target using either the outer edge of your thumb or the tip of your forefinger (or a crystal—more on that below). You want to apply significant pressure—you should feel the pressure intensely and deeply, but do ease up if you experience any pain. When you've finished targeting your pressure points, you should end any reflexology session with a series of feather-light touches up the feet, called "breeze strokes," to comfort the nerves.

Right before bed time is perfect for practicing reflexology on yourself (or your partner), as you'll likely find it very relaxing. You can finish up with some affirmations for rest, such as "I release today and rest my body, mind, and spirit for tomorrow."

Reflex Point Maps

Figures 13 and 14 below show the pressure points in the feet and hands and the organs and systems to which they correspond. While these may look intimidatingly complicated at first glance, don't worry—all you need to do is read these charts and find the areas on the feet and/or hands where pressure will target the organs or system of the body you're targeting for healing.

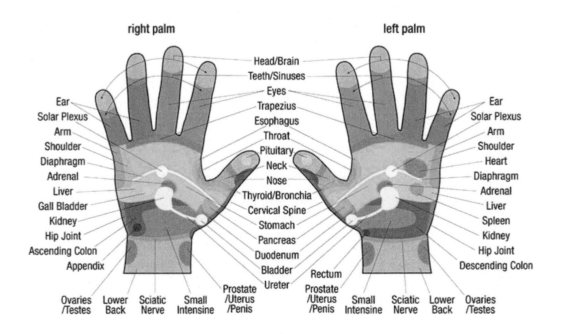

Figure 13: Reflexology map of the hands.

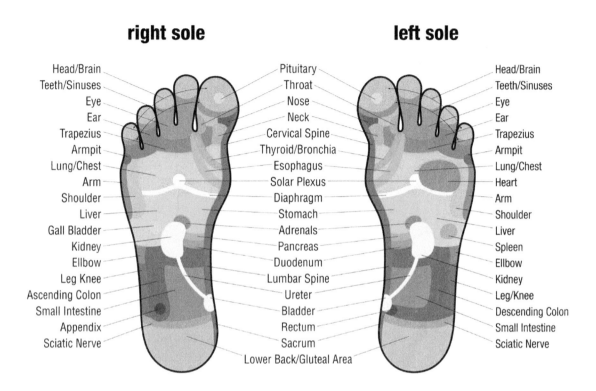

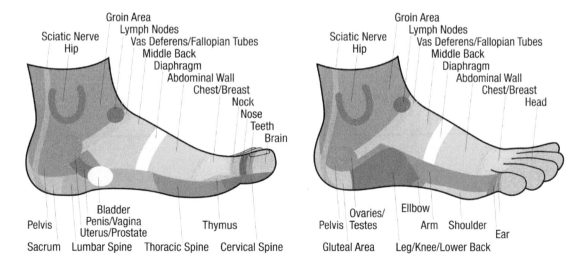

Figure 14: Reflexology map of the feet.

Using Crystals on Pressure Points

Healing stones are an incredibly simple way to both enhance and focus the benefits of reflexology. Using all you've learned throughout the book, you can trust your intuition (and reference the encyclopedia, as needed) to choose the crystals that correspond to particular ailments you want to address. Then, all there is to it is swapping your thumb or forefinger for the stone when applying pressure to the foot, as shown in Figure 15 below.

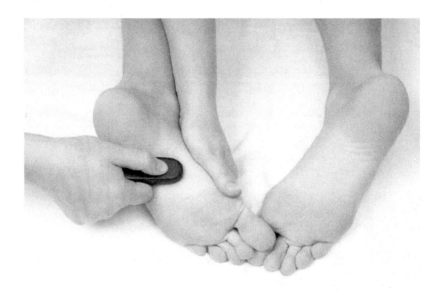

Figure 15: You can use a smoothed palm stone to place pressure on your reflexology points, sending that crystal's vibrations to heal the affected body systems.

Crystal Shapes in Reflexology Work

The greatest word of caution, here, is of course the *shape* of the stone you choose to use. **Under no circumstance should you press a sharply-edged crystal into a foot, hand, or any other body part.** A terminated quartz prism simply will not do here, nor a fluorite geode or pyrite cube. You should use only tumbled, polished, shaped stones for applying pressure in reflexology treatments.

Shaped and polished crystals come in a variety of forms, as you learned in Chapter 4. The best options for reflexology include wands with smooth terminations, spheres, eggs, and palm stones, as well as smaller, irregularly shaped tumbled stones.

Your "pointy" crystals are not useless in a reflexology practice, however. You can place crystals on or around the body while you work on the feet. I also find it valuable to meditate with crystals before my massage; this helps keep my chakras clear and open and my mind and body receptive to healing.

Take for example the problem of infertility. Moonstone, jade, and rose quartz are all excellent options, and specifically an egg-shaped stone will further amplify these crystals' fertility-awakening powers. Apply your crystal egg to the points on the charts above labeled as targeting the uterus and ovaries.

Palliative Care for Cancer Patients

Palliative care or supportive care is intended to improve quality of life for patients suffering serious medical problems. Rather than treating the disease or illness itself, palliative care aims to treat secondary symptoms, such as pain, to help the individual throughout the course of treatment.

I was lucky enough to avoid invasive medical treatments when battling my cancer, but not everyone has such a luxury. While chemotherapy and radiation therapy save lives, they come with a host of painful, difficult side effects: hair loss, nausea and vomiting, appetite loss, and extreme fatigue, to name a few. Fortunately, reflexology is ideal for treating these symptoms, and crystals can help.

Let's take a look at some of the best uses for reflexology regarding palliative care. This list of therapies is by no means exhaustive, but it should give you some ideas.

Peripheral Neuropathy

Some cancer treatments cause damage to peripheral nerves in the body, which carry information from the brain to other organs. These include sensory, motor, and autonomic nerves, and symptoms vary based on which nerves have been damaged:

- Sensory nerve damage causes tingling sensations, numbness, and inability to feel hot and cold temperatures on the body.
- Damaged motor nerves affect one's balance and mobility, making typical daily tasks feel impossible—leading to muscle atrophy in some cases.
- Damage to the autonomic nervous system can wreak all kinds of havoc, including low blood pressure, diarrhea, and sexual and urinary dysfunction.

Because reflexology directly manipulates the nervous system, it's an ideal treatment to relieve symptoms of peripheral neuropathy. To do so, refer to Chapters 3 and 4 to find stones that target the specific symptoms, then use them for reflexology massage. I recommend you repeat this therapy daily for the duration of cancer treatment.

Hand-Foot Syndrome

Redness, swelling, blisters, and pain in the soles of the feet and palms of the hands are the hallmarks of hand-foot syndrome (clinically called palmar-plantar erythrodysesthesia), a common side effect of cancer treatments. There is no treatment to resolve hand-foot syndrome, per se—instead, clinicians recommend ways to comfort the hands and feet, including pain relievers, ice packs, and moisturizing/exfoliating creams.

Luckily, reflexology, particularly when supplemented with crystals, can bring immense relief to these symptoms. If you have open sores on your feet, you should be particularly careful with this practice.

I recommend using calming stones and crystals known to soothe inflammation: blue lace agate, malachite, and lapis lazuli are perfect options. Try putting your crystals in the freezer for an hour or so before you use them on your feet and hands to provide additional cooling relief. A crystal roller wand (see Figure 16), typically marketed for facial skincare, can also be beneficial.

Figure 16: A rose quartz roller wand, especially if chilled, can be highly healing for hand-foot syndrome.

There is much more to reflexology than I've shared in this chapter. I hope you take what you've learned here and, if crystal reflexology brings you relief as it has for me, continue your practice on your own. You have all the knowledge you need to start; the rest is up to you!

Final Words of Gratitude

We've reached the end of this book. I am grateful to have accompanied you on the beginning of your crystal healing journey. Through these seven chapters, you've learned everything you need to build a crystal healing practice, from understanding what a crystal is and how it works to harnessing the healing energies of stones in all aspects of your life, together with complementary therapies. You're ready now to move beyond the basics; take what you've learned here and build on it through your own intuitive practice and further study.

As our time together ends, I want you to remember:

- When it comes to crystal healing, always trust your intuition over anything you find in a book. (And if you're not quite ready to trust your gut, work on opening those crown, third-eye, and solar plexus chakras!)
- The key to making crystal therapy work for you is to actively practice and grow. Build your practice through the methods I've described (and plenty more); don't let those crystals sit collecting dust on a shelf or stored away untouched in a box.
- There is no limit to the ways you can harness crystals and stones for healing. Don't wait until it's time to meditate. Keep your crystals close to you, use them in your home, office, and car, and share what you've learned (as well as your own personal crystals) with your loved ones to pay it forward.

The power is at your fingertips, ready for you to confidently wield. To the surprise of my medicine-minded parents, I am living proof of this! Have faith in yourself as I do—as the Universe does.

I will leave you with affirmations of gratitude.

I recognize the incredible gift that is my human body. No matter how ill or injured it may be right now, my body carries me forward toward healing.

I am grateful for my body's own capacity to heal itself. I am grateful for the life force energy running through me. I am grateful for my ability to harness this energy spiritually.

I thank my crystals for their generous exchange of energy, removing negatives from my mind, body, and spirit and imparting high vibrations.

I thank the Universe for my short, precious life, and this gratitude will propel me through the rest of my days filled with peace, joy, and serenity.

Thank you for purchasing this book. We at Intuitive Way would sincerely appreciate your honest feedback. Please leave us a review on Amazon as well as our website.

www.intuitive-way.com

Journal Page: Intentions & Affirmations

Write your own intentions and affirmations below for use with crystal meditation. I've given you a few examples to get your ideas flowing!

Let my spirit guides point me to the crystal I need right now.

With rose quartz, I give and receive love easily.

I'm worth the effort it takes to care for myself physically and spiritually.

Journal Page: Crystal Observations

Use this space to record your experiences with your crystals. Jot some notes down here whenever you add a new crystal to your collection or find a new use for one of your favorite stones.

I chose a tiger's eye palm stone today because I could feel it protecting me energetically when I picked it up. It fits with my goal to heal my solar plexus chakra—and it fits in my purse, too!

Glossary of Terms

Altar: A flat surface marked as sacred and decorated with spiritual or religious ornamentation and used for prayer or ritual, e.g. crystal altar.

Astral: As in *astral projection* or *astral travel*; describing an out-of-body experience of a spiritual nature in which the traveler enters the astral plane, often during sleep.

Attunement: In reiki, the process through which a practitioner's energy system is opened so as to better channel divine healing energies; the energetic ritual through which a reiki master initiates a practitioner.

Banding: Alternating layers of colors or minerals in a single cryptocrystalline stone.

Botryoidal: Describes a bumpy crystal shape composed of many rounded segments; *botrys* is Greek for "bunch of grapes."

Chakra: One of the seven major energy epicenters of the human body as written in the Vedic texts of ancient India.

Charging: The intentional passing of energies from a source to a destination, typically from a crystal to another object or medium, e.g. charged crystal water.

Cleavage: The tendency of a crystal to break along certain planes of symmetry when pressure is applied.

Crown: The 7th chakra, located at the top of the head and related to spirituality.

Crust: The topmost, solid layer of the earth, composed mainly of silicate minerals and much thinner than the mantle.

Cryptocrystalline: Describes a stone in which microscopic crystals have formed together into a cohesive whole. Here, the crystalline structure is not visible to the naked eye; see also *microcrystalline*.

Crystal Grid: A geometric arrangement of crystals to produce desired effects; typically, this is done on a square of cloth with a printed geometric grid.

Crystal System: A categorization of minerals that groups crystals by the geometry and symmetry inherent in their atomic structure; see also *lattice*.

Crystallization: The process through which crystals form; involves the melting and cooling or precipitation of constituent minerals.

Crystalline: Like a crystal; specifically, having a highly ordered molecular structure.

Cubic: Cube-shaped; one of the seven crystal systems.

Dendritic: Showing dendrites, or branching fractal patterns, e.g. tree branches, lightning burns.

Geode: A cavity in a rock lined with crystals that formed within that cavity.

Grounding: A spiritual practice of bringing your awareness into your body and taking power from your spiritual connection to the physical Earth.

Fluorescence: The emission of a visible glow under ultraviolet light.

Frequency: The number of energy waves (sound, electromagnetic, light, etc.) that pass a fixed point in a unit of time; a high-frequency equates to a shorter wavelength.

Habit: In crystallography, the characteristic macroscopic, external shape of a crystal, e.g. cubic, prismatic, tabular, massive, etc.

Hexagonal: Shaped like a hexagon, with six sides; one of the seven crystal systems.

Impurities: Elements in the crystal lattice of a mineral that are not constituents of that mineral's definitive chemical composition; e.g. manganese in quartz (silicone dioxide). Typical cause for color variation among mineral specimens.

Inclusion: One type of mineral crystal contained within another.

Lattice: The particular, orderly molecular structure of a mineral and its inherent symmetry, used to categorize a mineral into a *crystal system*.

Law of Vibration: A universal law that posits everything in the universe is in constant motion and vibrates at a specific frequency.

Lucid Dreaming: Dreaming while self-aware; often, a practice intentionally sought for the purpose of controlling what happens in one's dreams.

Magma: Molten rock underground; when magma erupts to the surface, it is called *lava*.

Mantle: The massive layer of molten rock between the Earth's crust (or surface) and its core.

Microcrystalline: A crystal whose structure is composed of many tiny crystals, such that the shape of the specimen at a macroscopic scale is not recognizable as a crystal *habit*; see also *cryptocrystalline*.

Mineral: A naturally occurring inorganic chemical solid; the constituents of crystals, stones, and rocks.

Monoclinic: Describes a rectangular prism with unequal sides; one of the seven crystal systems.

Orthorhombic: Describes a rectangular prism; one of the seven crystal systems.

Piezoelectricity: The electrical charge that accumulates in some materials (such as quartz crystal) when mechanical stress is applied.

Pineal Gland: A small endocrine gland in the human brain that regulates sleep and circadian rhythm; in energy healing, the pineal gland is associated with the third-eye chakra.

Prism: A three-dimensional geometric figure (polyhedron) in which the two ends are similar or identical and all sides are parallelograms.

Prismatic: Like a prism; used to describe the shape of a crystal.

Pyramid: A three-dimensional geometric figure (polyhedron) with one polygonal base and a point or apex where all sides meet; a common shape for crystals to be cut and polished into.

Reiki: A hands-on energy healing technique in which practitioners channel universal energy to administer healing; often assisted by crystals.

Root: The 1st chakra, located at the base of the spine and corresponding to one's basic sense of trust.

Sacral: The 2nd chakra, located two inches below the naval, governing sexuality and creativity.

Sphere: A three-dimensional circle; a common shape for crystals to be cut and polished into.

Silicate: A common type of mineral composed primarily of silica.

SiO$_2$: Also known as silica; silicone dioxide; the chemical composition of quartz mineral.

Solar Plexus: The 3rd chakra, located in the stomach and corresponding with power and self-esteem.

Tabular: Shaped like a table: flat and broad; describes one type of crystal shape.

Tetragonal: Describes a rectangular prism with two equal sides; one of the seven crystal systems.

Third Eye: The 6th chakra, located on the forehead and tied to awareness and intuition.

Triclinic: Describes a prism with three unequal vectors; one of the seven crystal systems.

Trigonal: Describes a prism with three equal axes; one of the seven crystal systems.

Vibration: A very fast, recurrent movement back and forth; refers to the motion of constituent particles that generates energy.

Wand: A cylindrical shape in which crystals are commonly cut and polished.

Notes and References

[1] Mafi, M. (2002, January 1). Rumi: Hidden music. Thorsons. ISBN-10: 000712032X.

[2] Tesla, N. (1900, June). The problem of increasing human energy: With special reference to the harnessing of the sun's energy. Century Illustrated Magazine, 60(2), 180.

[3] Power of crystals: Do they work, and how? (2019, August 23). Albiva. Retrieved from albiva.com/blogs/news/the-power-of-crystals-do-they-work-and-how.

[4] Frequently asked questions. (n.d.). Mineralogical Society of America. Accessed January 8, 2022, from http://www.minsocam.org/msa/collectors_corner/faq/faqmingen.htm.

[5] Moldavite healing properties, meanings, and uses. (n.d.). Crystal Vaults. Retrieved January 8, 2022 from https://www.crystalvaults.com/crystal-encyclopedia/moldavite/.

[6] Chrysoprase. (n.d.). Crystal Council. Retrieved December 20, 2021 from thecrystalcouncil.com/crystals/chrysoprase.

[7] Nunez, K. (2020, September 3). What is shungite and does it have healing properties? Healthline. Retrieved from https://www.healthline.com/health/shungite.

[8] Embong, N. H., Soh, Y. C., Ming, L. C., & Wong, T. W. (2015). Revisiting reflexology: Concept, evidence, current practice, and practitioner training. Journal of Traditional and Complementary Medicine, 5(4), 197–206. https://doi.org/10.1016/j.jtcme.2015.08.008

[9] Teagarden, K. (n.d.). What is the history of reflexology? University of Minnesota: Taking Charge of Your Health & Wellbeing. Retrieved January 9, 2022 from https://www.takingcharge.csh.umn.edu/history-reflexology.

Bedosky, L. (2020, May 13). All about reiki: How this type of energy healing works and its health benefits. Everyday Health. Retrieved from https://www.everydayhealth.com/reiki/.

Benefits of wearing crystal jewelry. (n.d.). Crystal Happenings. Retrieved December 10, 2021, from crystalhappenings.com/pages/why-wear-crystal-jewelry.

Crystal: Definition, types, structure & properties. (2016, June 11). Study.com. Retrieved from study.com/academy/lesson/crystal-definition-types-structure-properties.html.

Crystal grids 101: How to make a crystal grid to supercharge your life. (2020, February 22). Sage Crystals. Retrieved from sagecrystals.com/blogs/news/crystal-grids-101-how-to-make-a-crystal-grid.

Crystal structure. (n.d.). Byju's. Retrieved December 13, 2021, from byjus.com/chemistry/crystal-structure.

Crystals: The science behind the spiritual. (n.d.) ĀTHR Beauty. Retrieved December 11, 2021, from athrbeauty.com/blogs/goodvibesbeauty/crystals-the-science-the-spiritual.

Crystals and rocks. (2018, January 5). Crystal Healing London. Retrieved from crystalhealinglondon.com/2018/01/05/crystalsandrocks.

Curran, D. (2021, November 23). What is the universal law of vibration? And how it influences your life. Our Subconscious Mind. Retrieved from oursubconsciousmind.com/what-is-the-universal-law-of-vibration-and-how-it-influences-your-life.

Davis, F. (2020, November 14). Reiki crystals: How to choose, charge & use them for healing. Cosmic Cuts. Retrieved from https://cosmiccuts.com/blogs/healing-stones-blog/reiki-crystals.

Davis, F. (2020, November 20). How to use healing stones for distance healing. Cosmic Cuts. Retrieved from https://cosmiccuts.com/blogs/healing-stones-blog/distance-healing.

Davis, F. (2020, December 22). Crystals for dreaming: Amp up your dreamwork and have more lucid dreams. Cosmic Cuts. Retrieved from cosmiccuts.com/blogs/healing-stones-blog/crystals-for-dreaming.

Diaz, Robert. (2021, October 21). How to use reiki symbol stones the right way. Wellness Lens. Retrieved from https://wellness-lens.com/how-to-use-reiki-symbol-stones-the-right-way/.

Gemstone and crystal healing properties. (n.d.). Charms of Light. Retrieved December 12, 2021, from charmsoflight.com/gemstone-crystal-healing-properties.

Hand-foot syndrome or palmar-plantar erythrodysesthesia. (2019, June). American Society of Clinical Oncology. Retrieved from https://www.cancer.net/coping-with-cancer/physical-emotional-and-social-effects-cancer/managing-physical-side-effects/hand-foot-syndrome-or-palmar-plantar-erythrodysesthesia.

Healing properties and meanings of gemstones and crystals. (n.d.). InJewels Healing Jewelry. Retrieved December 10, 2021, from injewels.net/blogs/healing-properties-meanings.

How crystals are formed. (n.d.). Tiny Rituals. Retrieved December 13, 2021, from tinyrituals.co/blogs/tiny-rituals/how-crystals-are-formed.

How to choose the perfect healing crystal with your intuition. (n.d.). The Path Provides. Retrieved December 13, 2021, from thepathprovides.com/blog/how-to-choose-the-perfect-healing-crystal-with-your-intuition.

Langlais, S. (2020, February 19). The 3 levels of reiki: What are they & what do they mean? MindBodyGreen. Retrieved from https://www.mindbodygreen.com/0-16353/the-3-levels-of-reiki-what-are-they-what-do-they-mean.html.

Learn about crystals. (n.d.). The Crystal Council. Retrieved December 19, 2021, from thecrystalcouncil.com/crystals.

Magdalena, A. (n.d.). Crystal Combinations. Gemstagram. Retrieved December 20, 2021 from gemstagram.com/category/crystal-combinations.

Sharon Stone

Marie, T. (2010, October 29). Clear quartz crystals resonate with and amplify all energy frequencies. AngelLady Crystals. Retrieved from angelladytm.wordpress.com/2010/10/29/clear-quartz-crystals-resonate-with-and-amplify-all-energy-frequencies.

Murray, B. (2021, October 25). A beginner's guide to crystals. Harper's Bazaar. Retrieved from harpersbazaar.com/uk/beauty/fitness-wellbeing/a43244/crystal-healing-beginners-guide.

Peripheral neuropathy and cancer treatment. (2020, January 15). National Cancer Institute. Retrieved from https://www.cancer.gov/about-cancer/treatment/side-effects/nerve-problems.

Oakes, L. (n.d.). Kundalini awakening: How does it aid enlightenment? Healing Crystals for You. Retrieved January 8, 2022 from https://www.healing-crystals-for-you.com/kundalini-awakening.html.

Patel, R. (2020, February 21). Warning signs your chakras are out of balance. MindBodyGreen. Retrieved from https://www.mindbodygreen.com/0-13433/warning-signs-your-chakras-are-out-of-balance.html.

Pine, J. (n.d.). Where to place crystals in your home for the best energy. Better Homes & Gardens. Retrieved December 13, 2021, from bhg.com.au/where-to-put-crystals-in-your-home-for-the-best-energy.

Regan, S. (2021, May 18). Kundalini awakening: Signs, causes & how to cultivate kundalini energy. MindBodyGreen. Retrieved from https://www.mindbodygreen.com/articles/kundalini-awakening.

Scialla, J. (n.d.). A brief history of crystals and healing. Crystal Age. Retrieved December 13, 2021, from crystalage.com/crystal_information/crystal_history.

Science behind healing crystals explained. (2019, August 1). The Times of India. Retrieved from timesofindia.indiatimes.com/life-style/health-fitness/home-remedies/the-science-behind-healing-crystals-explained/articleshow/70482968.cms.

Top 10 healing crystals for beginners and their benefits. (n.d.). Desert Citizen. Retrieved December 12, 2021, from desertcitizen.com/blogs/style/top-10-healing-crystals-for-beginners-and-their-benefits.

Weingus, L. (2018, May 8). Reiki symbols & their meanings: Everything you need to know. MindBodyGreen. Retrieved from https://www.mindbodygreen.com/articles/reiki-symbols-meanings.

Yugay, I. (2019, January 27). How to identify the symptoms of blocked chakras. MindValley Blog. Retrieved from https://blog.mindvalley.com/symptoms-of-blocked-chakras/.

Zarifian, P. (2017, September 10). Health benefits of reflexology. Bao Foot Spa. Retrieved from https://www.baofootspa.com/blog/2017/9/10/benefits-of-reflexology.

Zoldan, R. (2020, June 22). Your 7 chakras, explained—plus how to tell if they're blocked. Well + Good. Retrieved from wellandgood.com/what-are-chakras.

Printed in Great Britain
by Amazon

79602846R00095